Beginners Guide to Knitting by Pictures

Learn to Knit with Simple Step-By-Step Instructions and Full Picture Illustrations

By

Maggie Samir

Copyright © Autumn Leaf Publishing Press, 2019

Email: Publisher@AutumnLeafPub@gmail.com

All Rights Reserved.

Without limiting the rights under the copyright laws, no part of this publication may be reproduced, stored in or introduced into a retrieval system, or transmitted, in any form or by any means (electronic, mechanical, photocopying, recording or otherwise), without the prior written consent of the publisher of this book.

Autumn Leaf Publishing Press publishes its books and guides in a variety of electronic and print formats, Some content that appears in print may not be available in electronic format, and vice versa.

Design & Illustration by Rebecca Johnson

First Edition

Contents

THE ART OF KNITTING ....- 4 -

    MASTERING THE SLIP KNOT ....- 5 -

    HOW TO CAST ON ....- 12 -

        Long Tail Cast-On ....- 12 -

        The Cable Cast-On ....- 19 -

KNIT THE BASIC STITCHES: ....- 27 -

    THE KNIT STITCH ....- 27 -

    THE PURL STITCH ....- 31 -

    THE SLIP STITCH ....- 37 -

EDGING STITCHES ....- 38 -

    THE KNOTTED EDGE ....- 38 -

    THE CHAIN EDGE ....- 39 -

    THE SEAM EDGE ....- 40 -

KNITTING WITH DIFFERENT NEEDLES ....- 41 -

    THE MAGIC LOOP ....- 42 -

    DOUBLE POINTED NEEDLES ....- 48 -

HOW TO INCREASE IN KNITTING ....- 61 -

    MAKE ONE (M1) ....- 61 -

        M1 R (make one, right) ....- 61 -

        M1 L (make one, left) ....- 63 -

    YARN OVER (YO) ....- 65 -

    KNIT FRONT BACK (KFB) ....- 69 -

    ADD AT THE BEGINNING OF A ROW ....- 71 -

HOW TO DECREASE IN KNITTING ....- 74 -

- Knit Together (K2tog) .... - 74 -
- Slip, Slip, and Knit (SSK) .... - 76 -

HOW TO BIND OFF KNITTED STITCHES .... - 80 -

MORE COMMON STITCHES .... - 85 -
- The Garter Stitch .... - 85 -
- Stockinette Stitch .... - 87 -

RIB STITCHES .... - 91 -
- Single Rib Stitch .... - 91 -
- Dual Rib Stitch .... - 95 -
- Two to One Rib Stitch .... - 97 -

SHAPED STITCHES .... - 100 -
- Square Stitch (2x2) .... - 100 -
- Horizontal Rectangle Stitch .... - 105 -
- Vertical Rectangle Stitch .... - 109 -
- Triangle stitch .... - 115 -
- Strips Stitch .... - 128 -
- The Seed Stitch .... - 132 -
- Barely Stitch .... - 135 -

CABLING STITCHES .... - 146 -
- Basic (Braid) Cable Stitch .... - 146 -
- Double Cable (Horseshoe) Stitch .... - 162 -

CONCLUSION .... - 173 -

The Art of Knitting

Knitting is a beautiful way to create amazing works of art like scarfs, sweaters, blanket, socks, dresses, and more. The only limit is your imagination.

Mainly knitting consists of stitches made by a special needle. The length of a standard needles ranges from 30 to 40 cm and are numbered by size. There are circular needles as well as double pointed needles. Knitting needles are sold in packs of five. The size of the needle corresponds with the type of yarn.

Mastering the Slip Knot

In order for the knitting piece to match the desired shape, it is necessary first to make a sample of about 20-30 stitches and measure the length of these stitches.

Completing this step indicates the number of stitches you need to cast on.

To start knitting, make a slip knot.

Step 1: Hold the end of the yarn with your left hand.

Step 2: Then wrap the tail in the shape of a circle.

Step 3: Pick up the yarn inside the loop.

Step 4: Pull it through, but do not tie it in a tight knot just yet.

Step 5: Put the needle inside the knot.

Step 6: Then pull the end of the yarn to tighten the knot.

Alternatively, you can use this second method for creating a slip knot.

Step 1: Wrap the yarn around your finger two times.

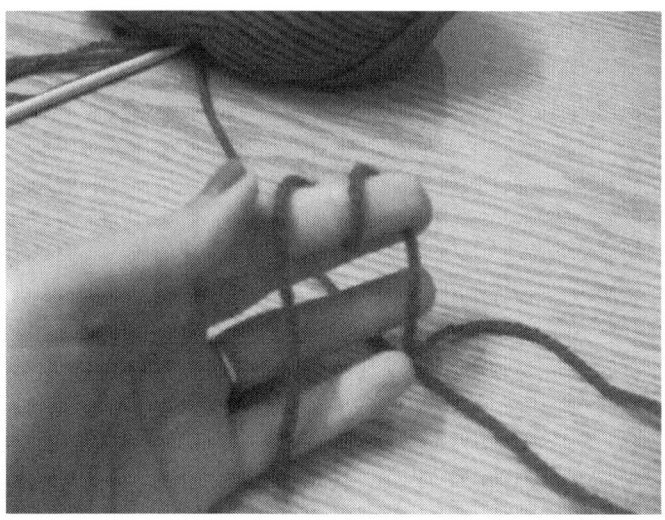

Step 2: Then pull the back loop over the front loop.

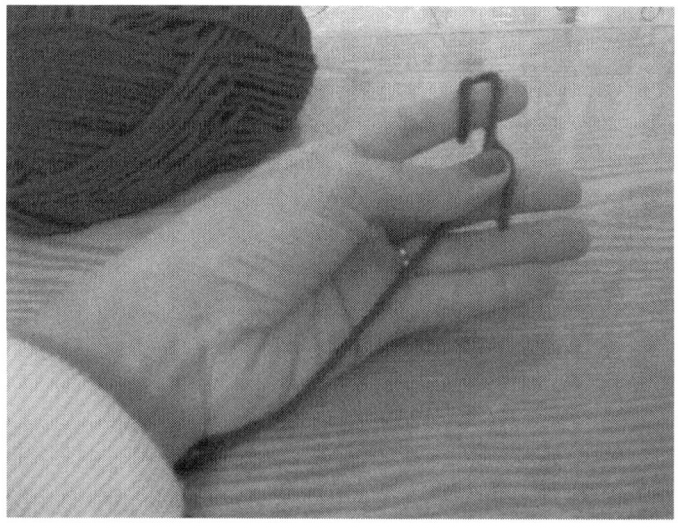

Step 3: Pull the new back loop over off of your finger.

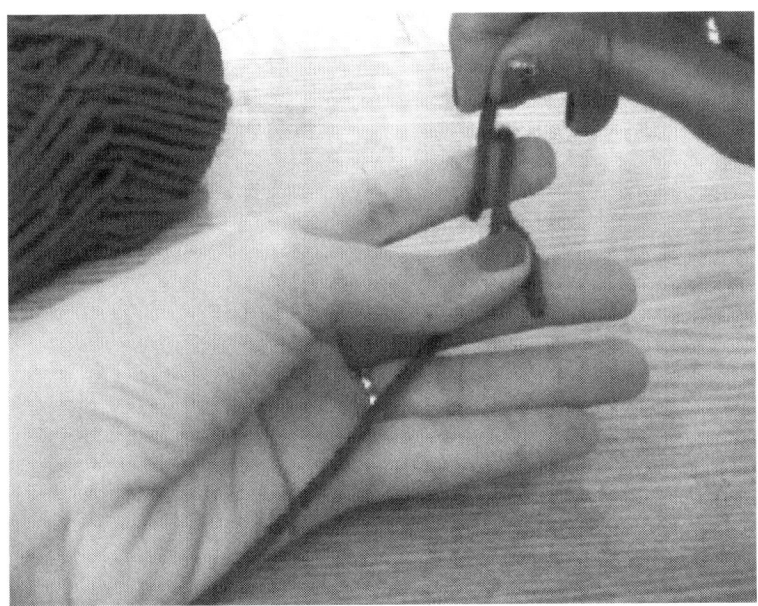

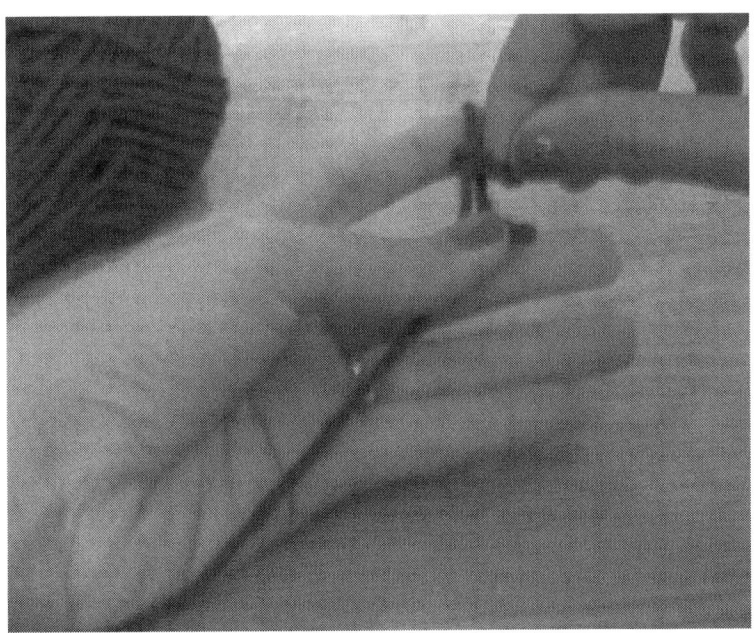

Step 4: Tighten the knot.

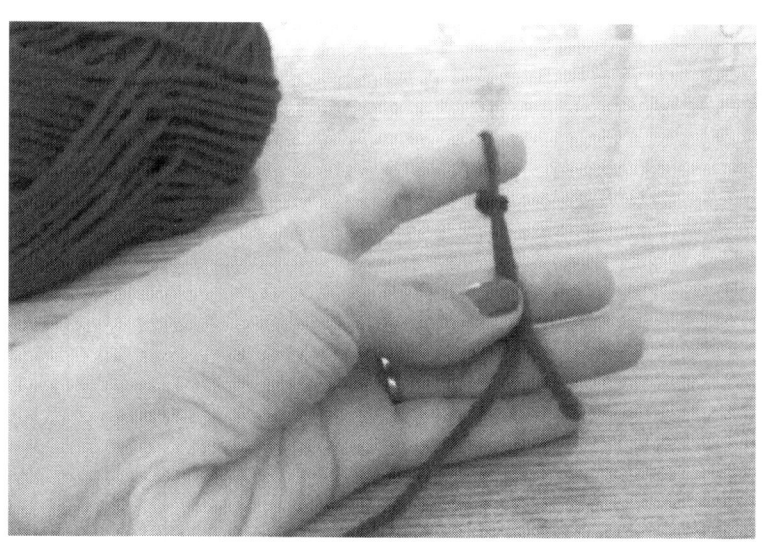

Step 5: Slip the knot onto a knitting needle.

How to Cast On

Casting on in knitting means creating the first stitches of your project, or creating stitches that are not dependent upon other stitches.

Long Tail Cast-On

The first method of casting on requires only one knitting needle. This method is mostly known as "long tail cast-on."

It is very common and is a simple method to give you an even and elastic edge to begin your knitting piece.

First, you have to estimate the amount of yarn you will need for your cast-on. You will need 2.5cm (almost 1 inch) for each stitch, so if you need to cast 5 stitches, you have to leave 12.5 cm (about 5 inches) of your yarn.

Example: 2.5cm x 5 stitches = 12.5cm

Step 1: Grip your yarn and make a slip knot at a suitable distance proportional to the number of stitches you want to cast-on.

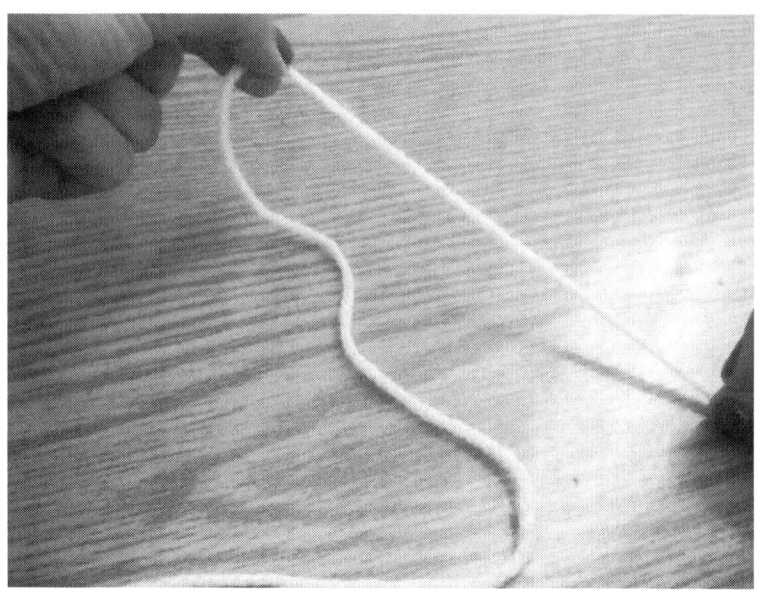

Step 2: Creating a triangle with the slip knot at the top of the triangle, take the tail and drape it over your thumb.

Take the working yarn and drape it over the other finger for the other side of the triangle.

Step 3: The last three fingers will grip the working yarn and the tail to pull them tight.

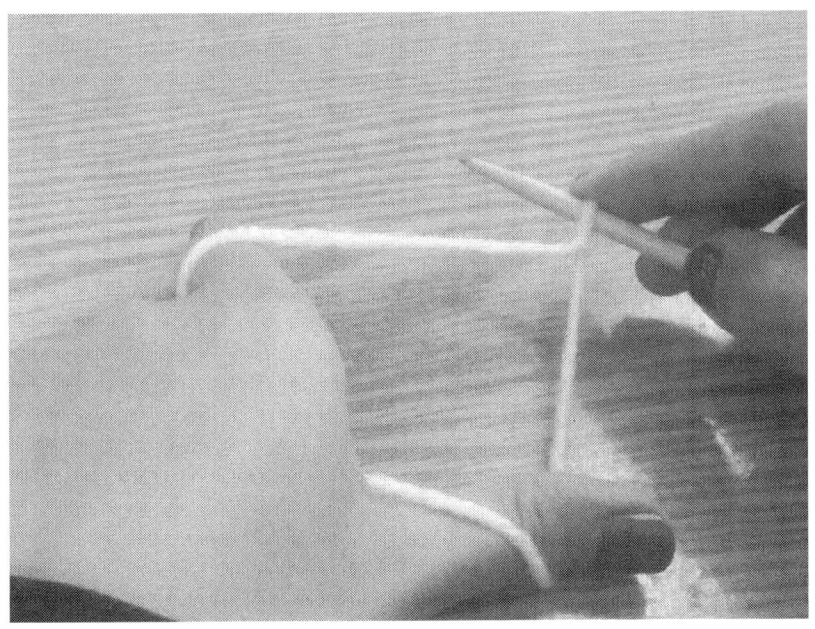

Step 4: Move the needle from the bottom to the top by your thumb.

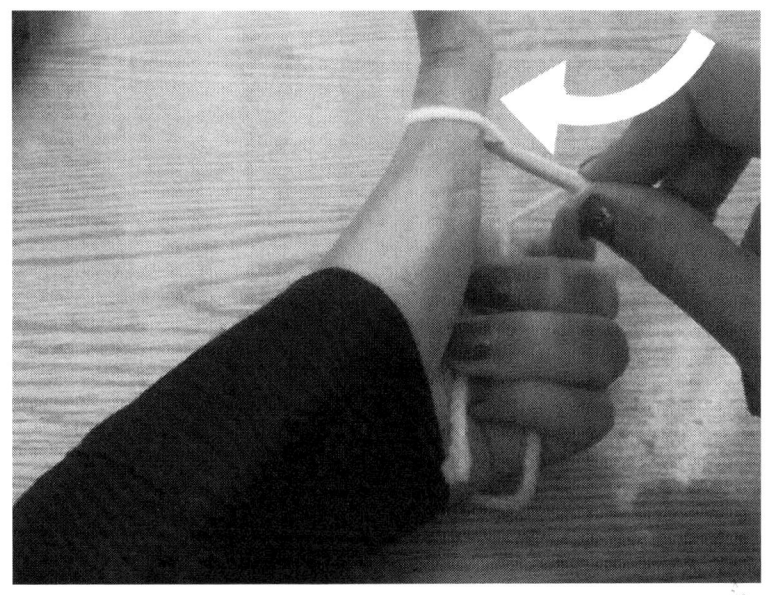

Step 5: Go up to the bottom by your pointer finger.

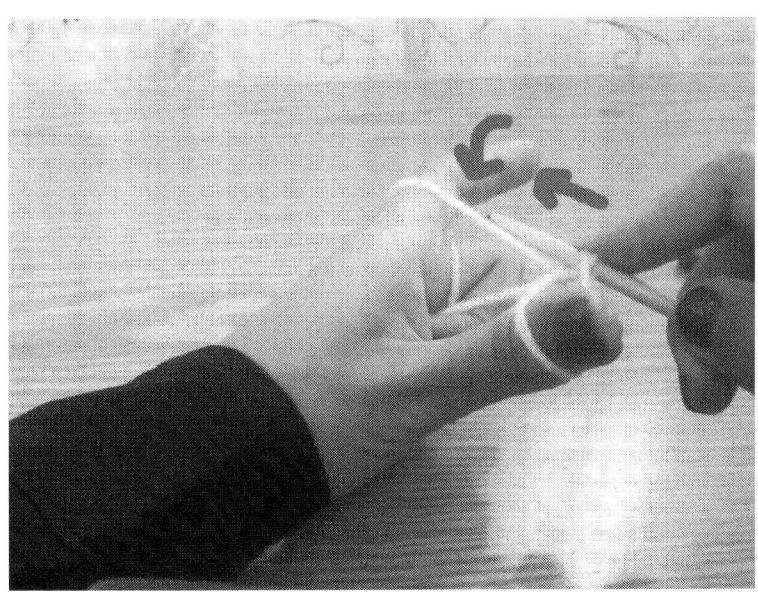

Step 6: Go back to the same loop by your thumb and move from top to the bottom.

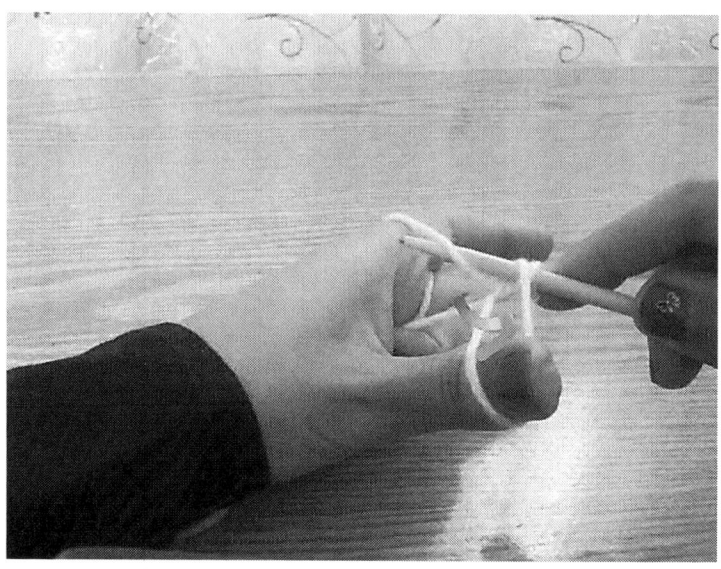

Step 7: Then let go with your thumb and use your thumb to pull the stitch tight.

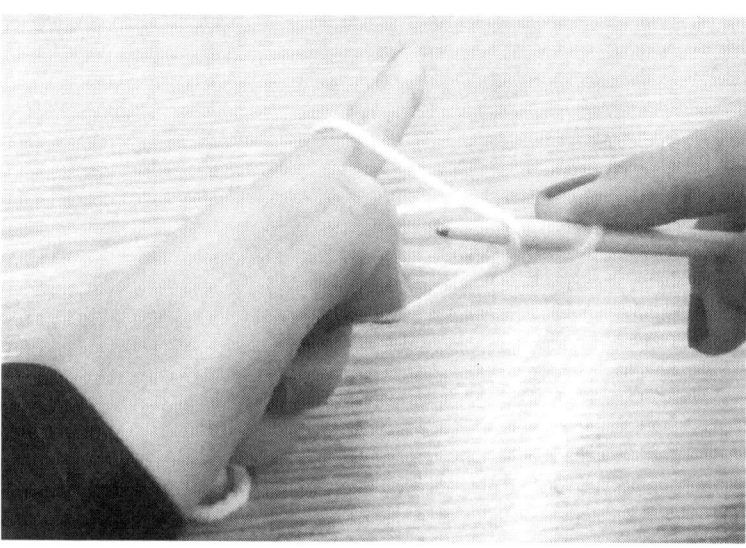

Step 8: Continue casting in this manner.

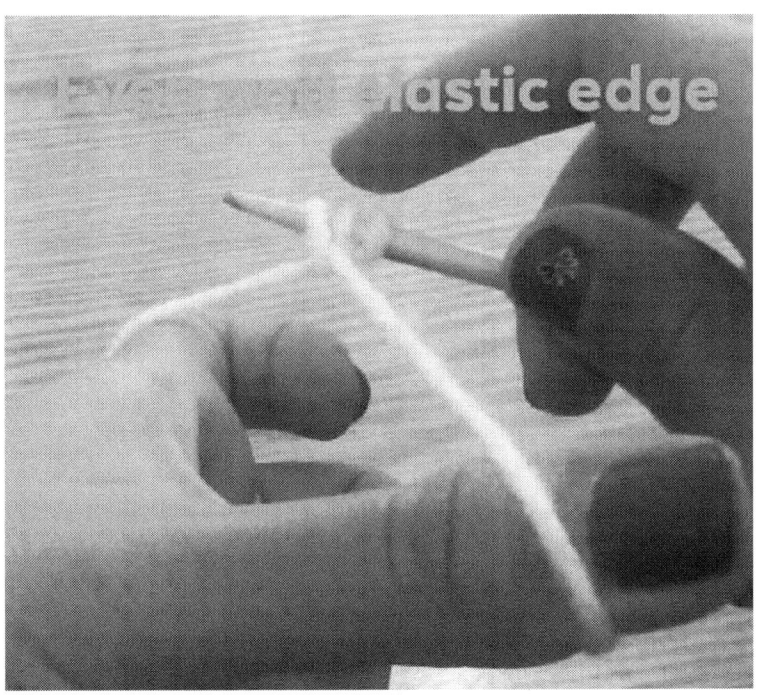

- 18 -

The result is an even and elastic edge to begin your knitted piece.

Next, we will examine the cable cast on method.

The Cable Cast-On

The second method of casting on requires two knitting needles. This is known as "cable cast-on." It is really easy for beginners to learn.

This method gives you a regular even edge, and the stitches will be more elastic than the first method.

Step 1: Grip your yarn and knitting needles firmly, then make a slip knot on the left-hand needle.

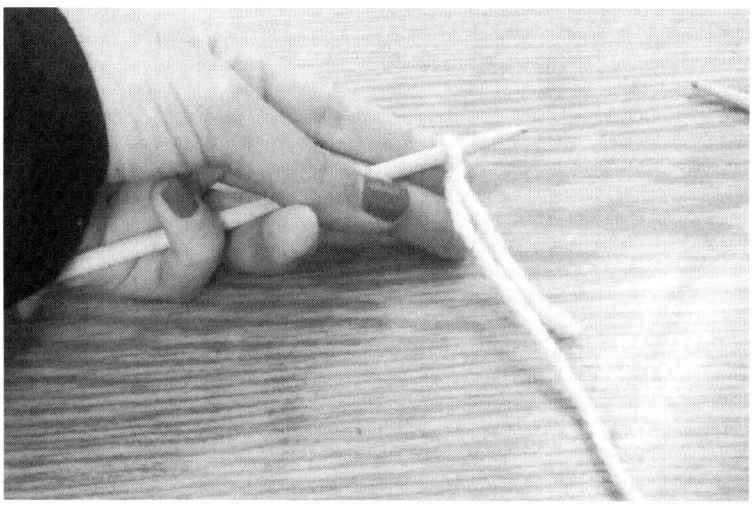

Step 2: Use your right-hand needle to go into the stitch from the bottom to the top, so your right needle is beneath the left needle.

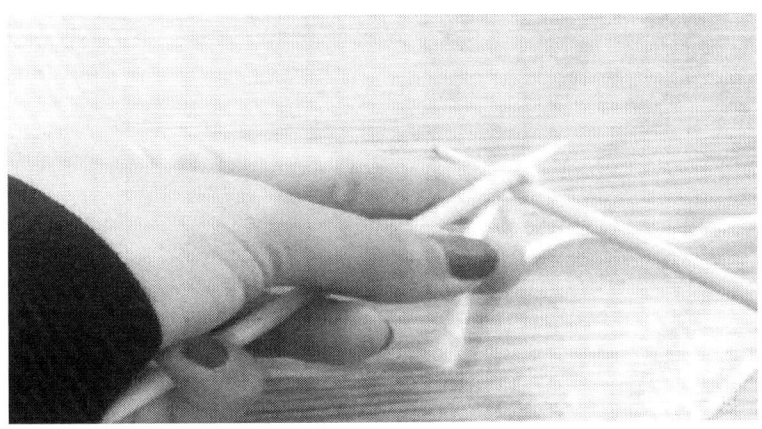

Step 3: Grip the working yarn with your right hand and put it in between your two needles then wrap it around your right-hand needle.

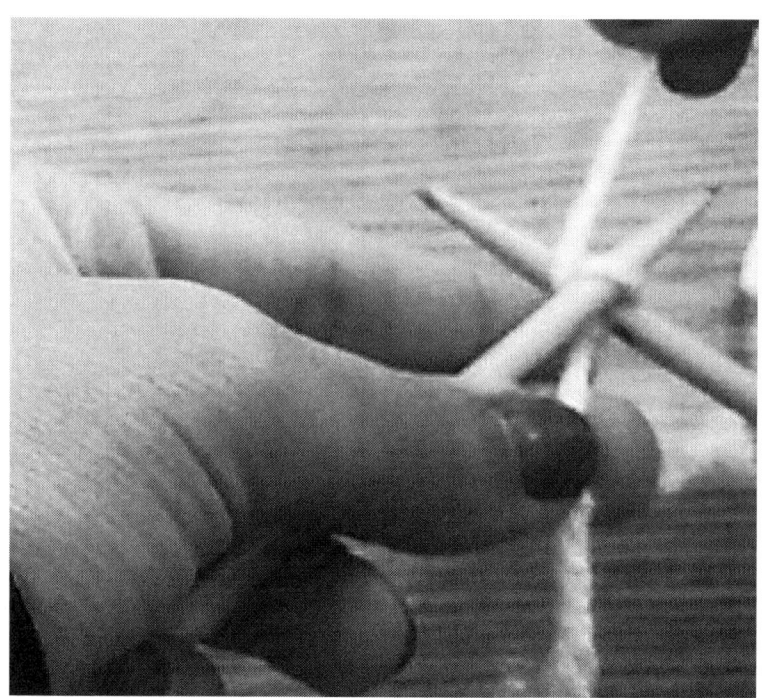

Step 4: With the right-hand needle go back through the same stitch from top to bottom.

Step 5: Pick up the wrapped yarn and pull it with your right-hand needle.

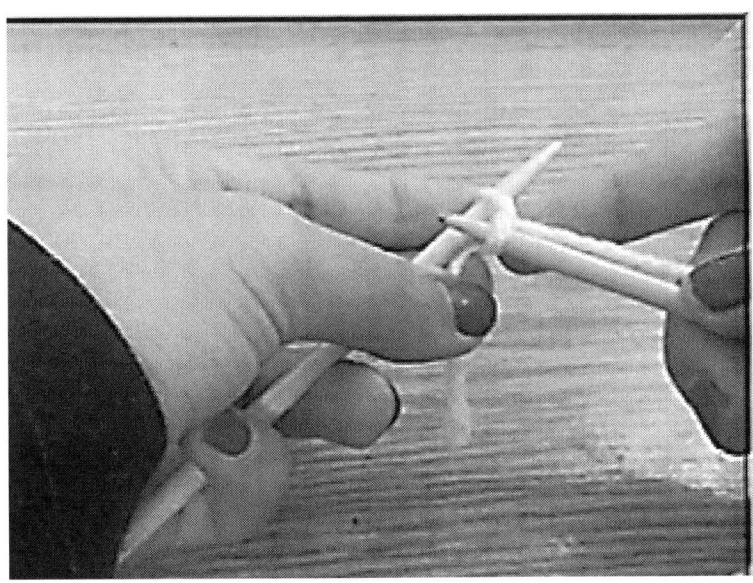

Step 6: With your left-hand knitting needle go into the stitch from the bottom to the top and slip it onto your left-hand needle.

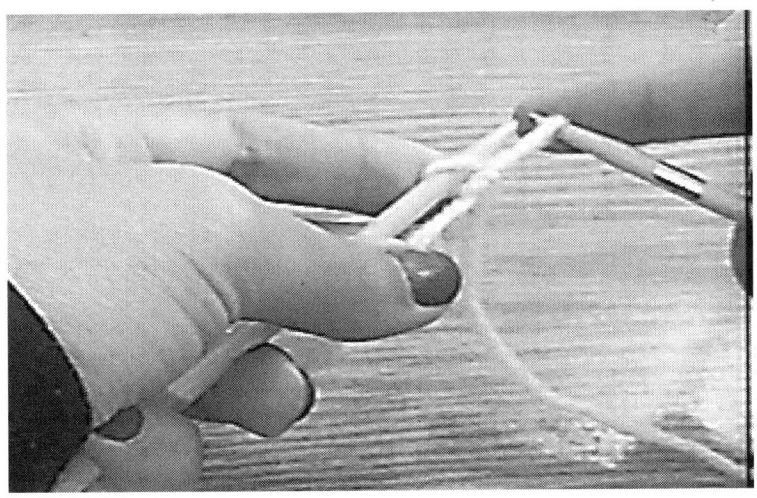

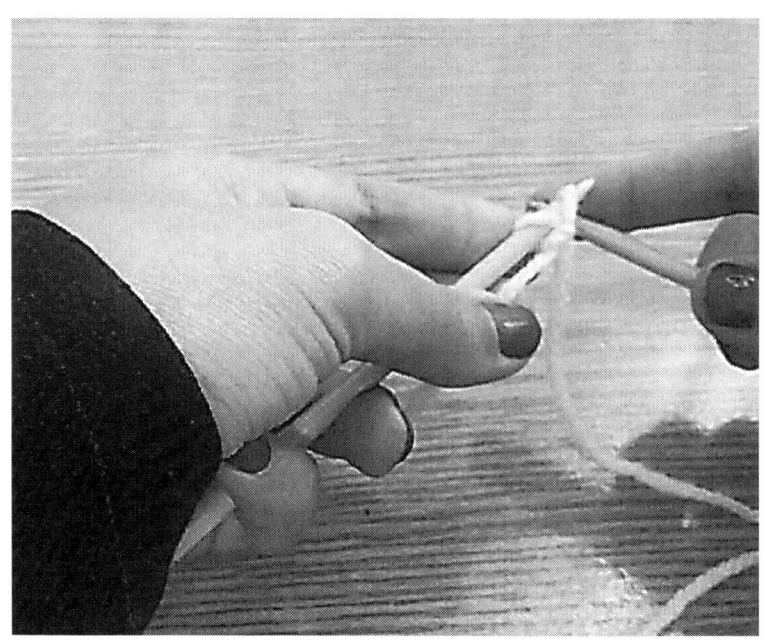

Step 7: Now, you have two stitches on your left needle. With your right needle go in between the two stitches, so the right needle is beneath the left needle.

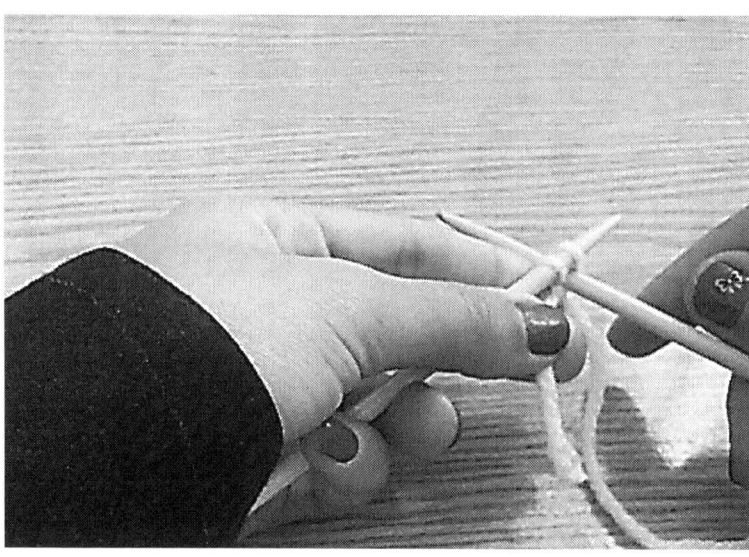

Step 8: Grip the working yarn around your right needle.

Step 9: Take your right needle and go back through the same stitch from the back to the front.

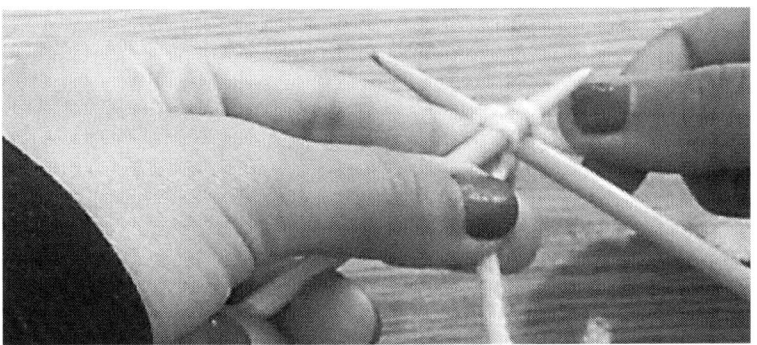

Step 10: Pick up the wrapped yarn and pull it with your right-hand needle.

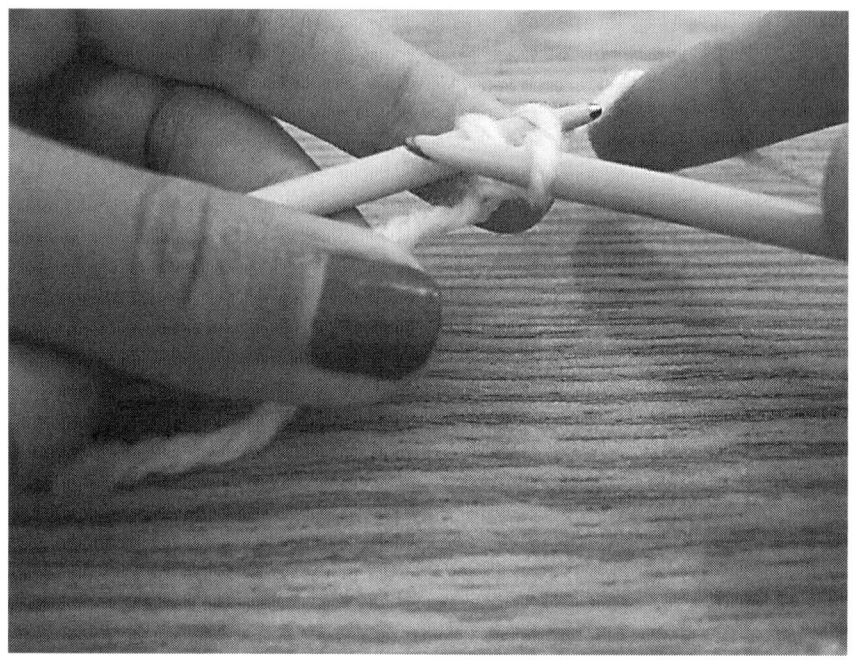

Step 11: Now, you have two stitches on your left needle and one on your right needle.

Step 12: Take your left needle and go through the stitch from the bottom to the top and slip the stitch onto your left needle.

Repeat the steps to cast more stitches.

Go in between the last two stitches and grip the working yarn around your right needle. Work back through the same stitch from the back to the front. Take your left needle and go into the stitch from the bottom to the top. Keep going until you have the number of stitches you need for your pattern.

Knit the Basic Stitches

There are three basic stitches, the knit stitch (K), the purl stitch (P) and the slip stitch. We will first examine how to make the knit stitch.

The Knit Stitch

To make the knit stitch, follow these basic steps.

Step 1: Make a slip knot and then cast on the number of stitches that you need according to your pattern. You can cast on using any method you choose.

Step 2: Put your right-hand needle into the first stitch on your left needle from the bottom to the top (up).

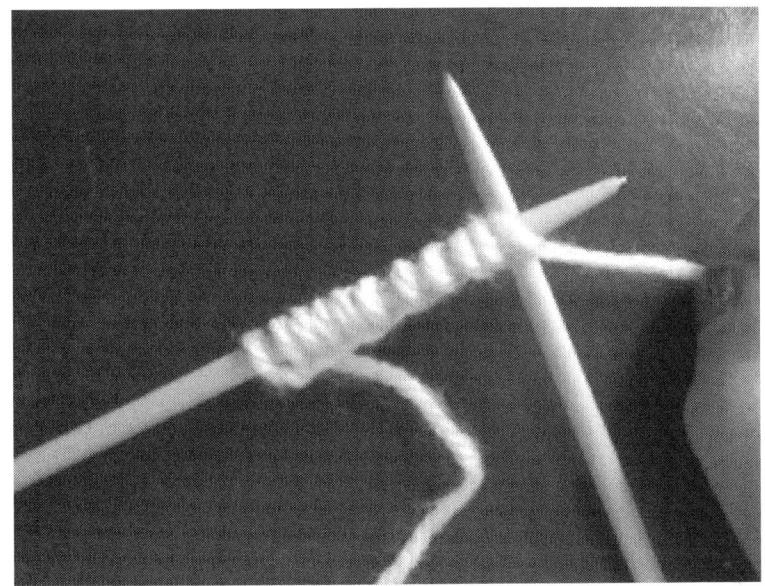

Step 3: Pick up your working yarn with your right hand, put the thread in between the two needles. Wrap the thread around your right-hand needle.

Step 4: Take your right needle and go back through the same stitch from top to bottom (down), now you have the stitch on your right-hand needle.

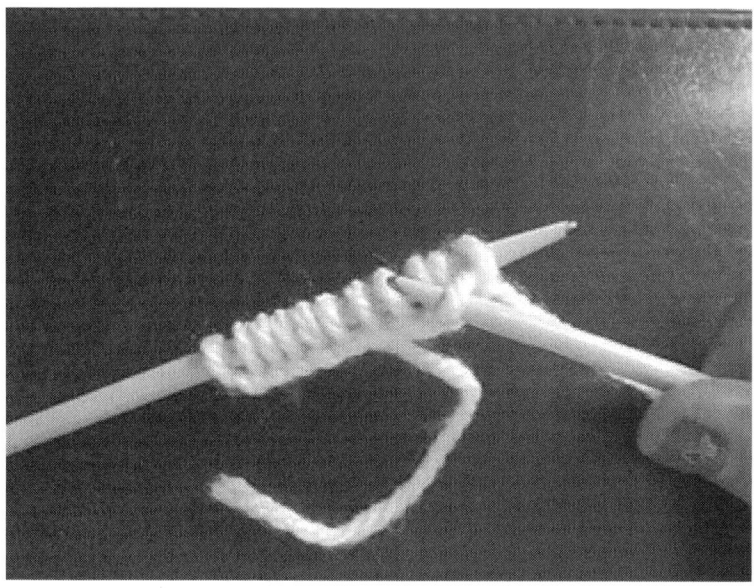

Step 5: Slip the stitch off of your left-hand needle.

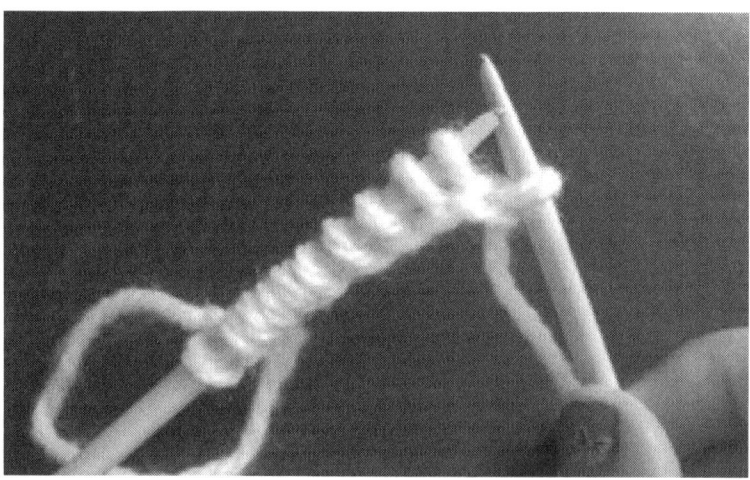

The stitch is now on your right-hand needle.

Step 6: Repeat these steps all the way down the row until you complete each stitch.

After you finish knitting your first row, you will notice that the right-hand needle has all the stitches on it and the left-hand needle does not have any stitches.

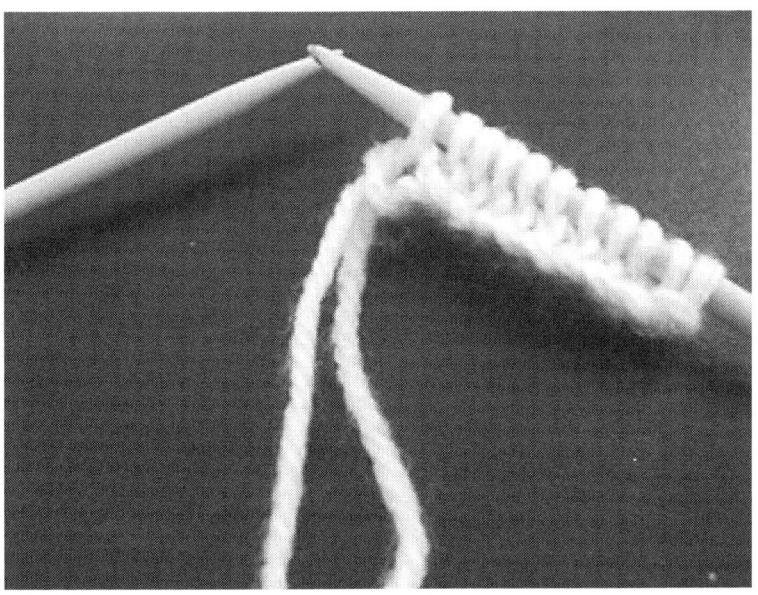

To continue knitting the next row, turn the work. Switch your needles. This means that the right-hand needle that has all the stitches on it will be the left-hand needle. The left-hand needle that does not have any stitches will be your right-hand needle.

The Purl Stitch

The purl stitch is the opposite of the knit stitch.

Step 1: To begin the purl stitch, make a slip knot. Then cast on the number of stitches that you need according to your pattern. You may use any method to cast on the stitches.

Step 2: Pick up your right-hand needle and put it into the first stitch on your left-hand needle from top to bottom (down).

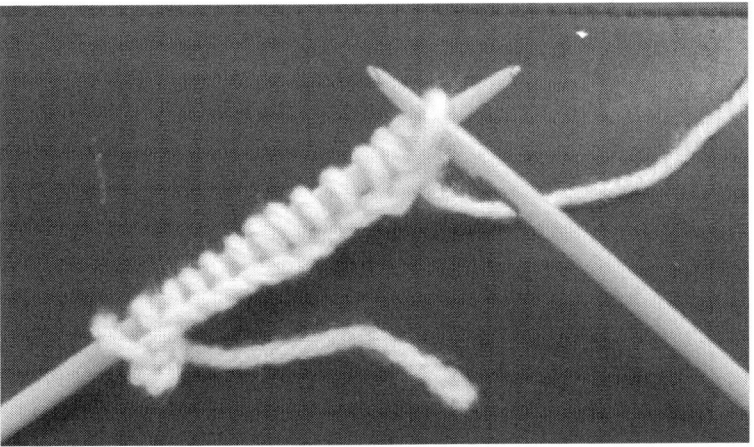

Step 3: Pick up your working yarn with your right hand and put the thread in between your two needles.

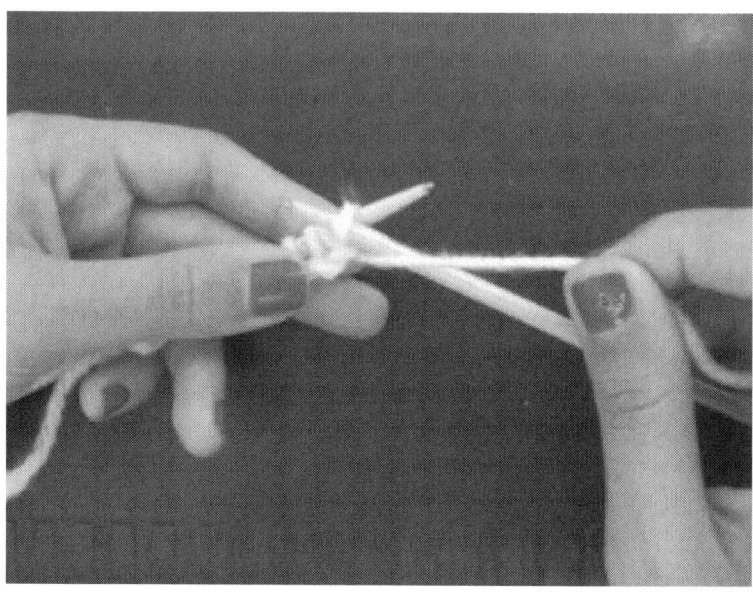

Step 4: Then wrap it around your right-hand needle.

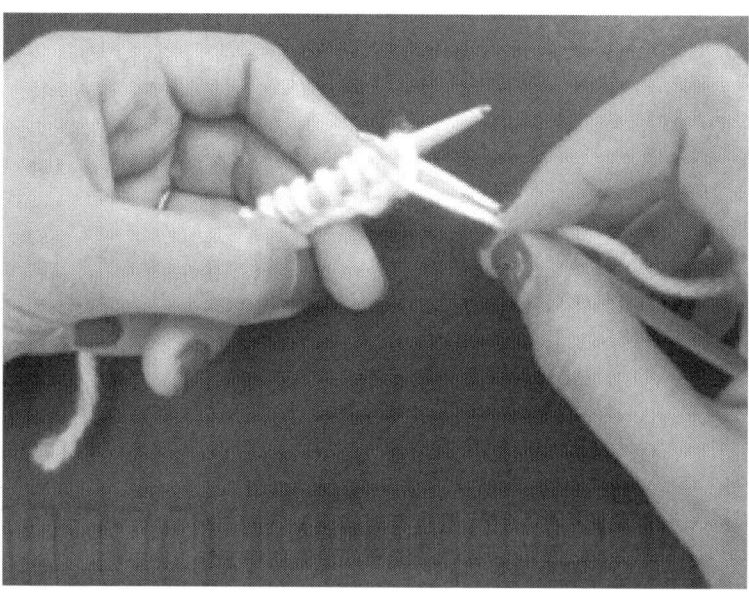

Step 5: Take your right-hand needle and go back into (through) the same stitch from the bottom to the top (up), now you have the stitch on your right-hand needle.

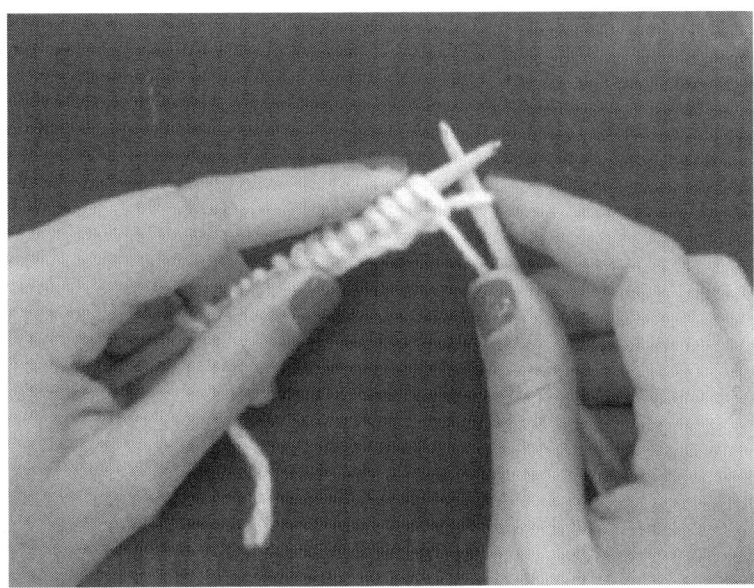

Step 6: Slip the stitch off of your left-hand needle.

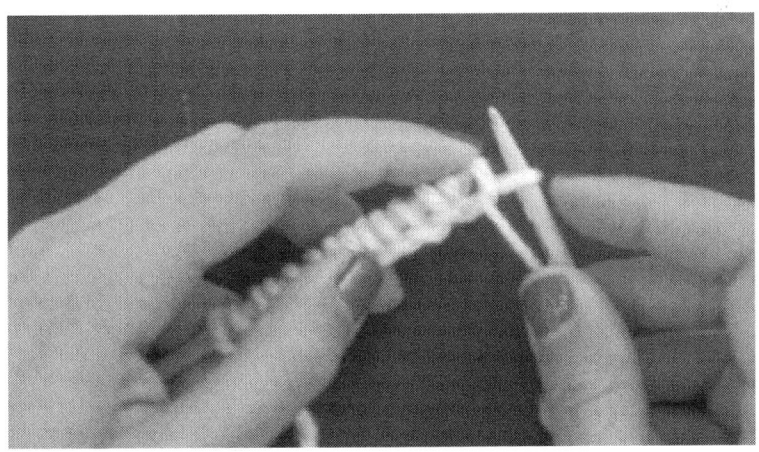

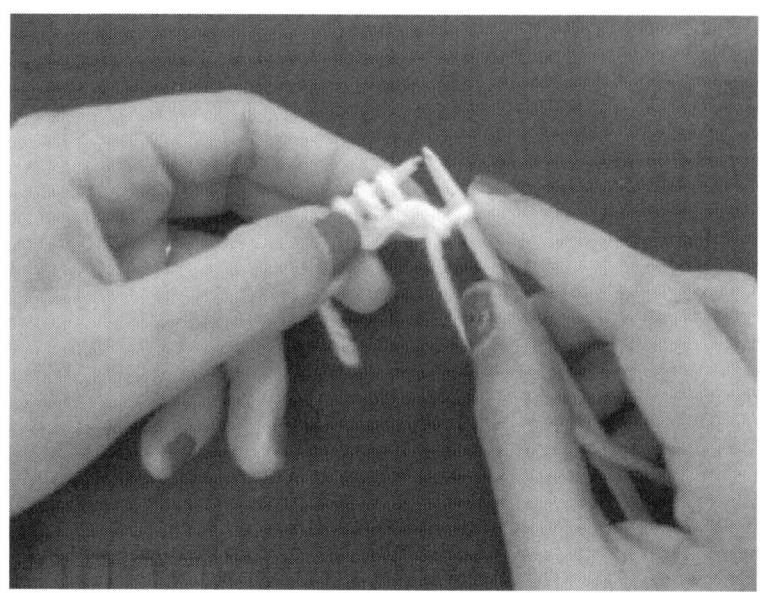

Step 7: Continue repeating these steps all the way down the row until you complete each stitch.

After you finish purling your first row, you will notice that the right-hand needle has all the stitches on it and the left-hand needle does not have any stitches.

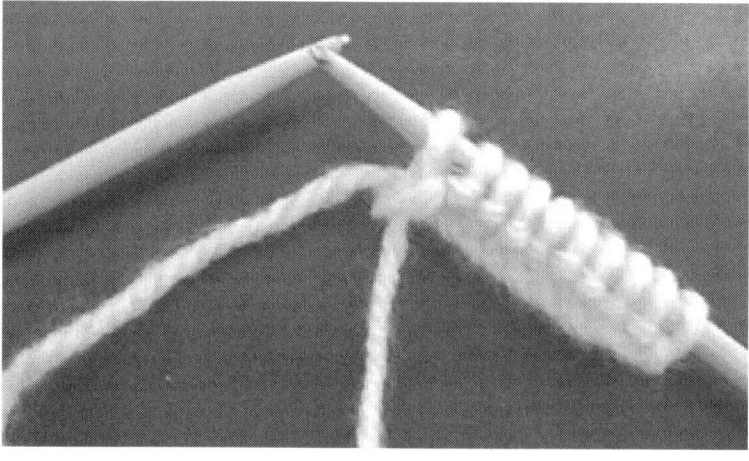

Step 8: To continue knitting the next row, turn your work. Switch your needles.

The needle that has stitches on it will be the left-hand needle. The needle that does not have any stitches on it will be your right-hand needle.

Step 9: Continue with this manner until you finish your pattern.

The Slip Stitch

To create a slip stitch, you have to transfer the stitch from your left-hand needle into your right-hand needle without knitting or purling it and without twisting it.

To make a slip stitch in knitting, insert your right needle into the stitch on your left-hand needle from the front to the back.

Slip it off your left-hand needle onto your right-hand needle. To make a slip stitch in purling, insert your right needle into the stitch on your left-hand needle from the back to the front. Slip it off your left-hand needle onto your right-hand needle.

Edging Stitches

There are a few ways to do an edge stitch. The methods we will explore include the knotted edge, the chain edge, and the seam edge.

The Knotted Edge

Complete the first and the last stitches on a row with a knitted stitch. It gives you a loose edge.

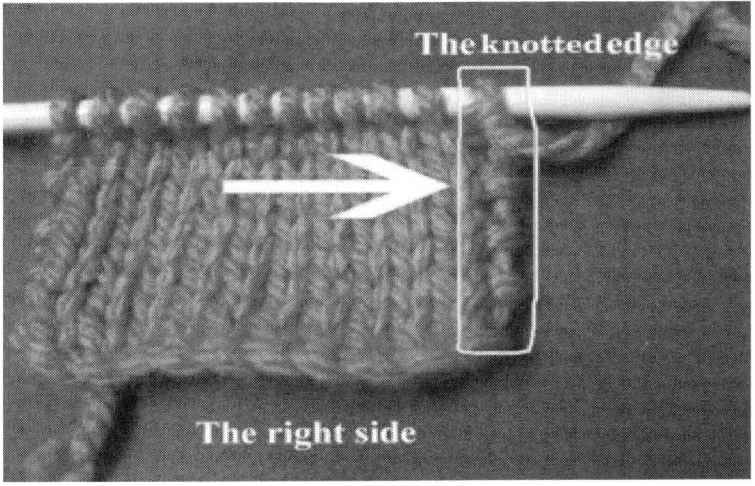

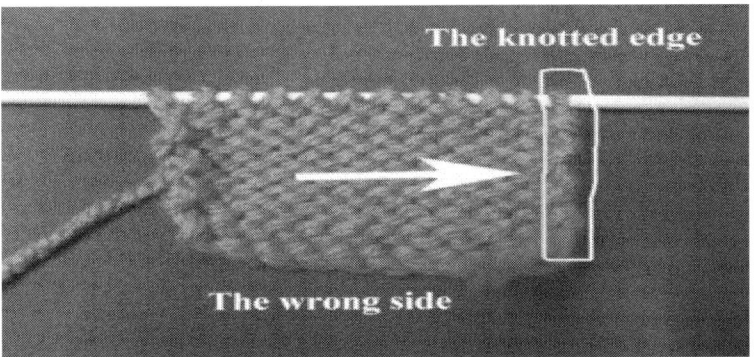

The Chain Edge

Slip the first stitch and knit the last stitch in each row. This results in a smooth edge.

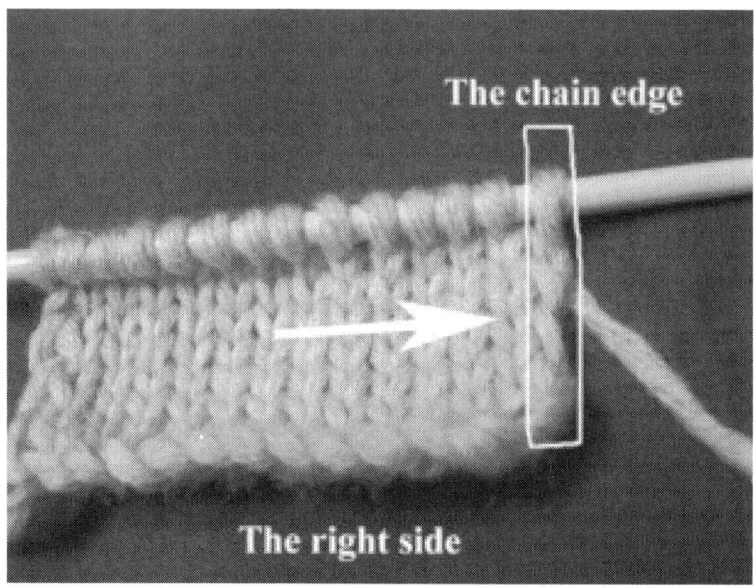

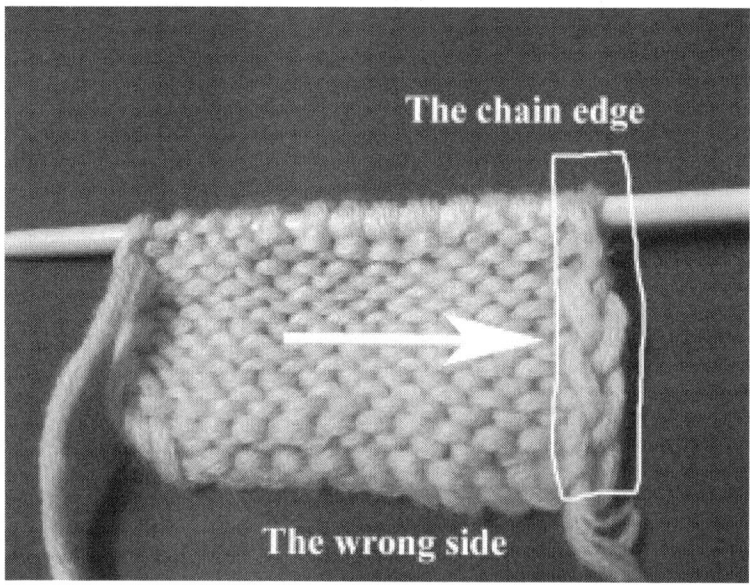

The Seam Edge

This edge is perfect if you are going to connect one piece to another. On the right side knit the first and the last stitch. On the wrong side purl the first and the last stitch.

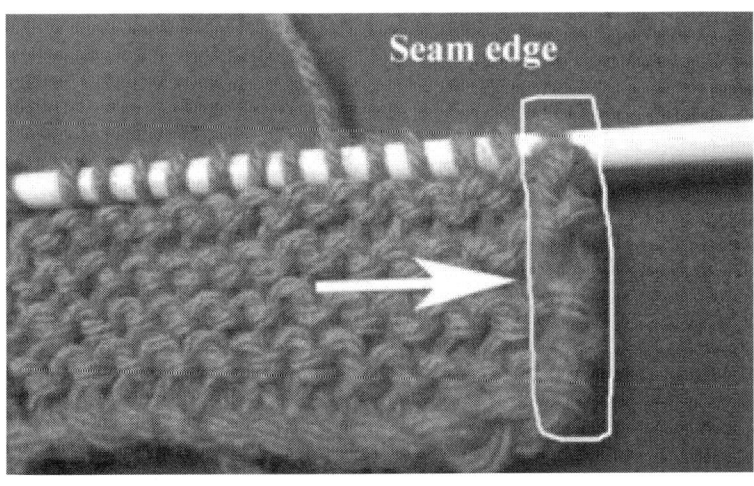

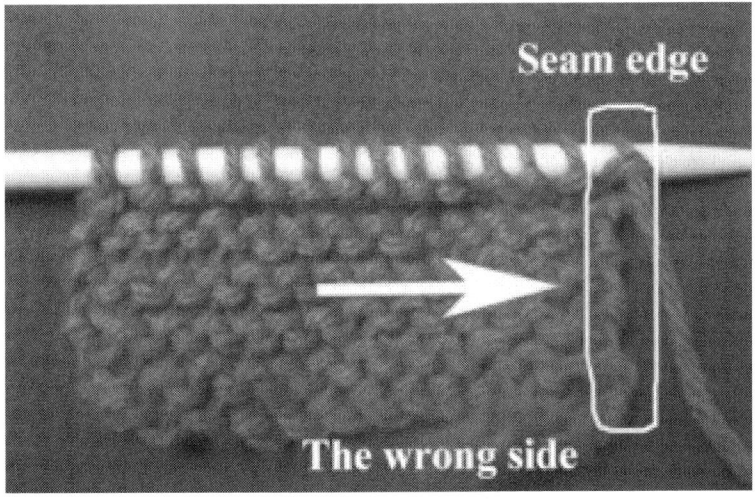

Knitting with Different Needles

There is more to knitting than just using the standard straight set of needles. In this chapter, we will explore other types of needles- the magic loop and double pointed.

Many new knitters get confused as to when to use a double-pointed needle and when to use a circular needle. Let's examine the differences between these two needles.

Double-pointed needles are really amazing for smaller knitted projects like gloves and fingerless gloves. This is because the smallest circular needle available is 16 inches in circumference.

Typically, you want your needle to be smaller than the finished circumference of whatever it is that you are going to knit. Items smaller than 16 inches in circumference will need to be knitted with a double-pointed needle.

Circular needles are great for in-the-round projects. It comes in an array of sizes to fit large knitting projects. It is easier to hold onto a circular needle.

The Magic Loop

A circular needle is also called a "Magic Loop."

This circular needle is two needles connected with an acrylic plastic loop.

The magic loop allows stitches to be created in a round rather than back and forth.

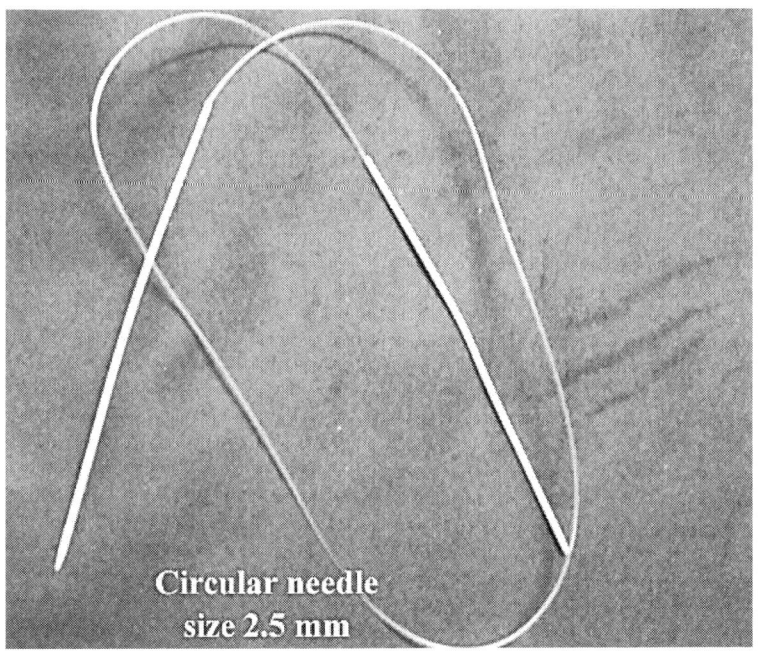

A circular needle is perfect for making hats and sleeves.

It comes in different sizes just like a regular needle, but it also comes in different lengths.

Circular needles come in 16, 24 and 36-inch lengths. So be careful when choosing your needles according to the pattern instructions.

Try to choose a needle length (circumference) that is smaller than the finished circumference of whatever it is that you are going to knit.

Step 1: Make a slip knot and then cast the number of stitches that you need for your pattern. Pull the stitches all the way around the circular needle.

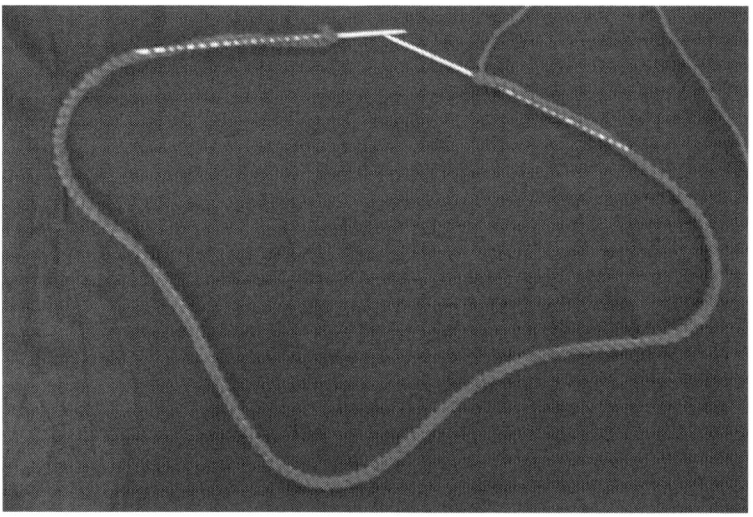

The working yarn should be on the right-hand needle, make sure that all stitches are straight or not twisted. This means that the edge of your knitting is facing inwards of the circle.

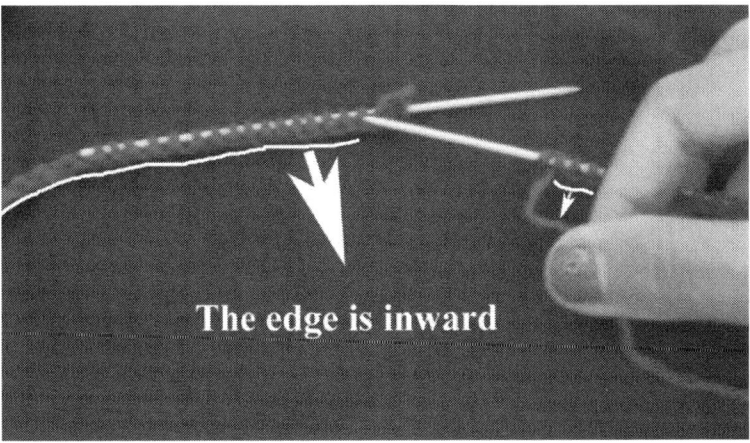

Step 2: Put a stitch marker between the first and the second stitch to mark the beginning of your round.

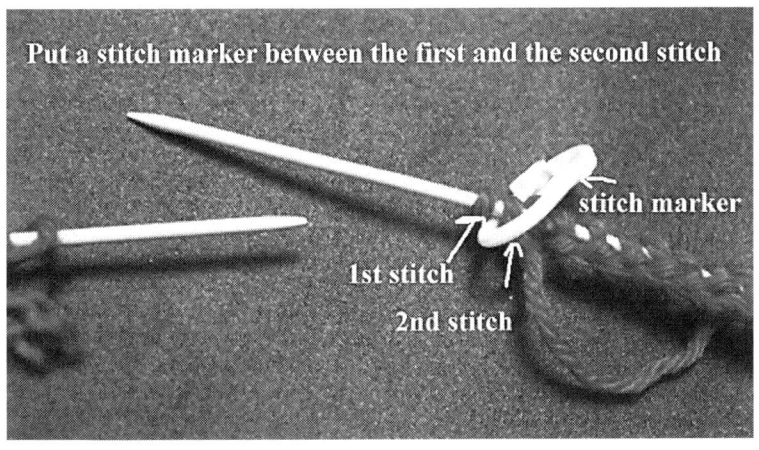

Step 3: To join the round, knit the first stitch by using the working yarn.

Use the tail to secure it and pull it tight. Be sure not to form a gap.

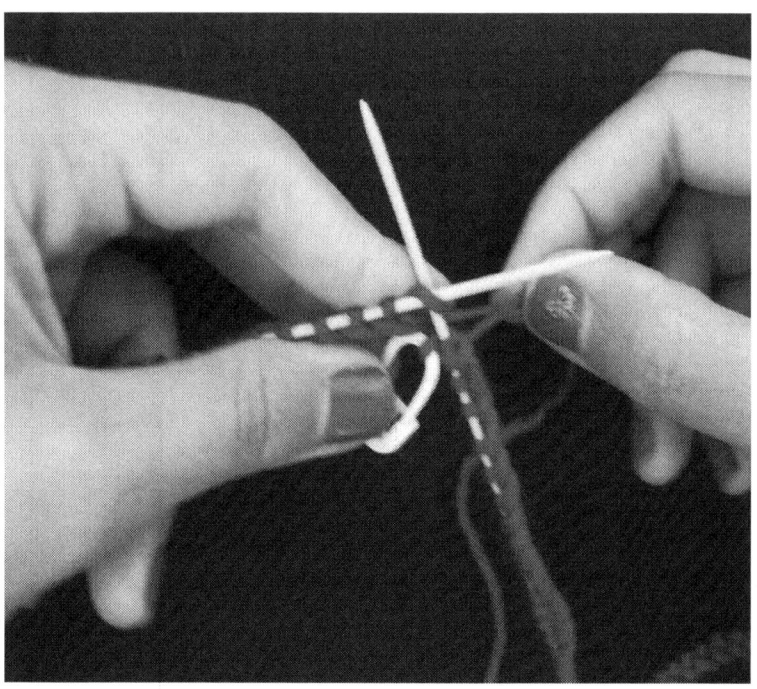

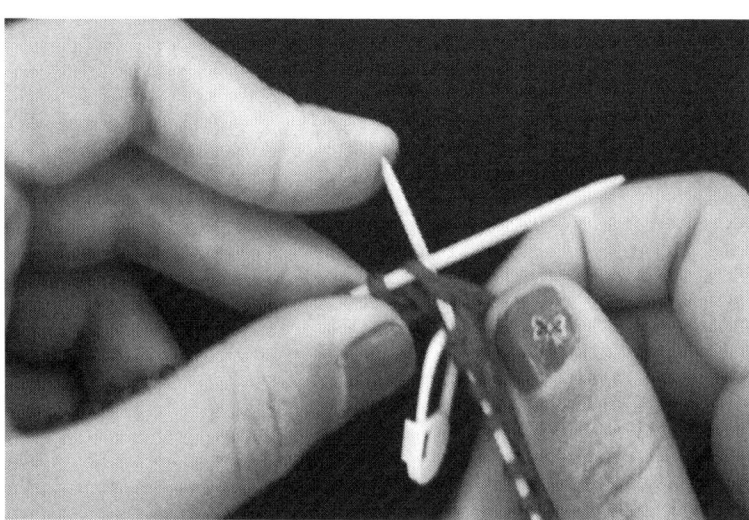

Step 4: Cut the tail to hide it. Continue knitting all the way around with the working yarn until you reach the marker. Slip the marker onto the right-hand needle.

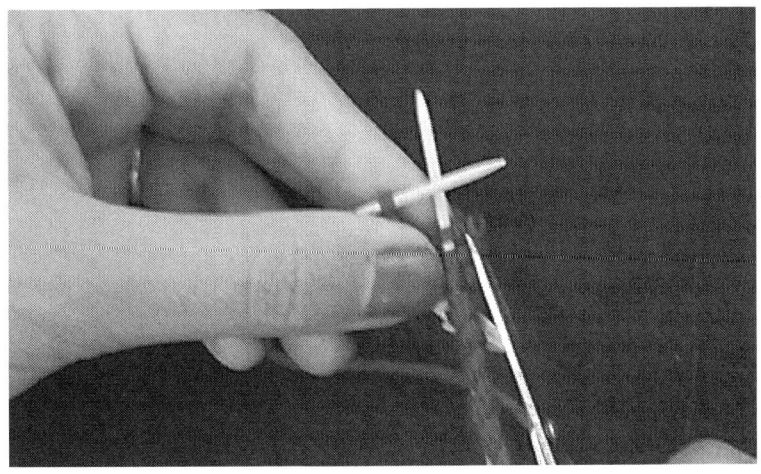

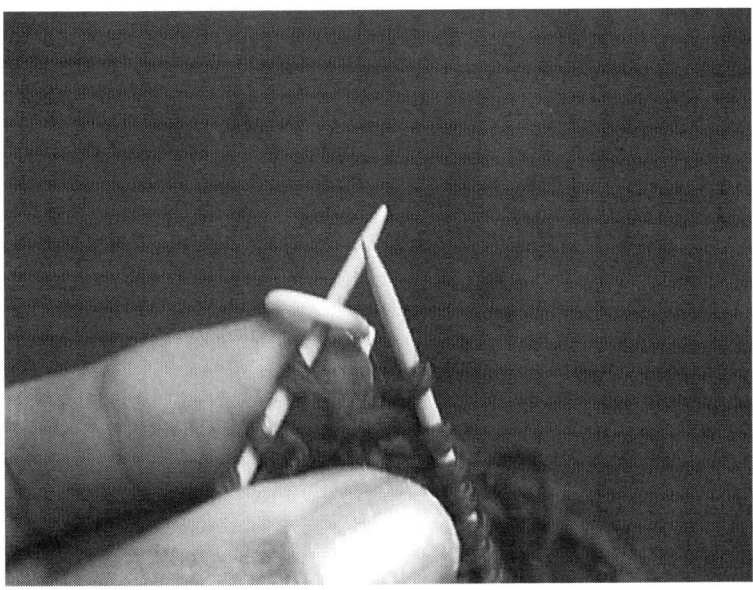

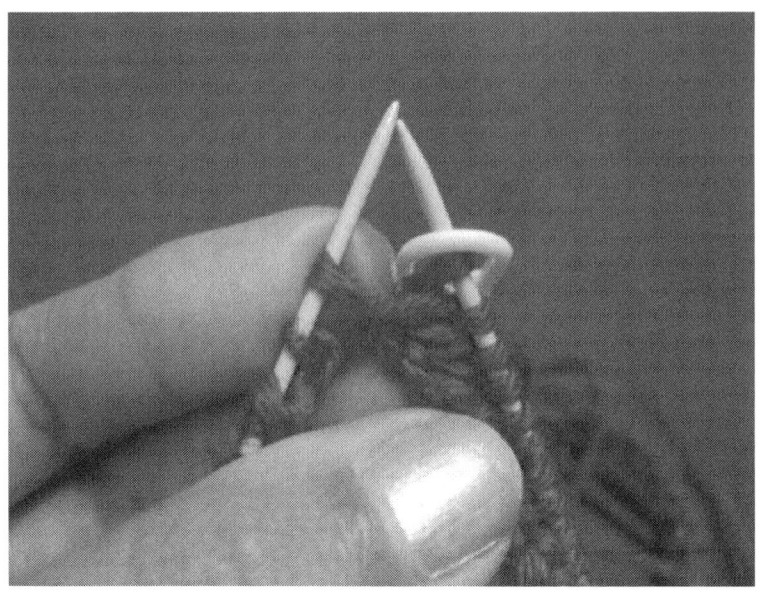

Step 5: Start round two, keep going around until you reach the desired length.

Double Pointed Needles

Double pointed needles are amazing for many projects like gloves and fingerless gloves.

They are available in packs of 5 needles.

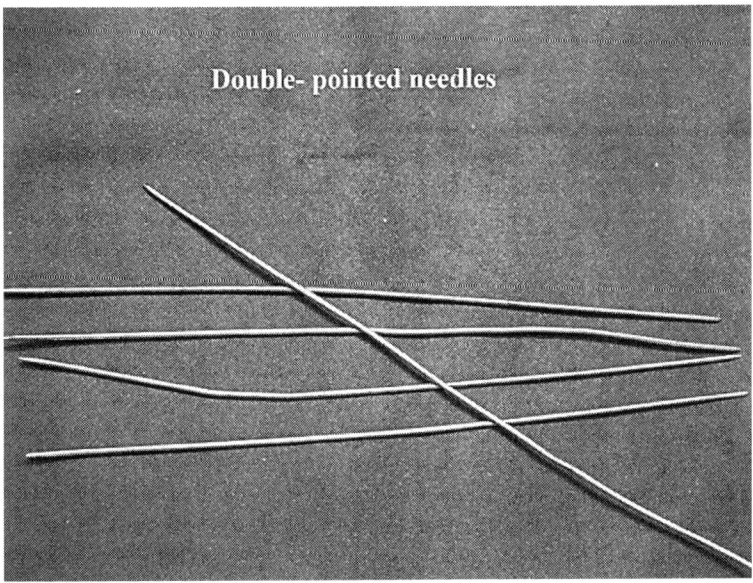

They have numbers like regular needles, so make sure you get the right size for your pattern and yarn.

To knit with double-pointed needles, follow these simple instructions.

Make a slip knot then cast on the desired number of stitches needed for your pattern. You can use any casting method you prefer.

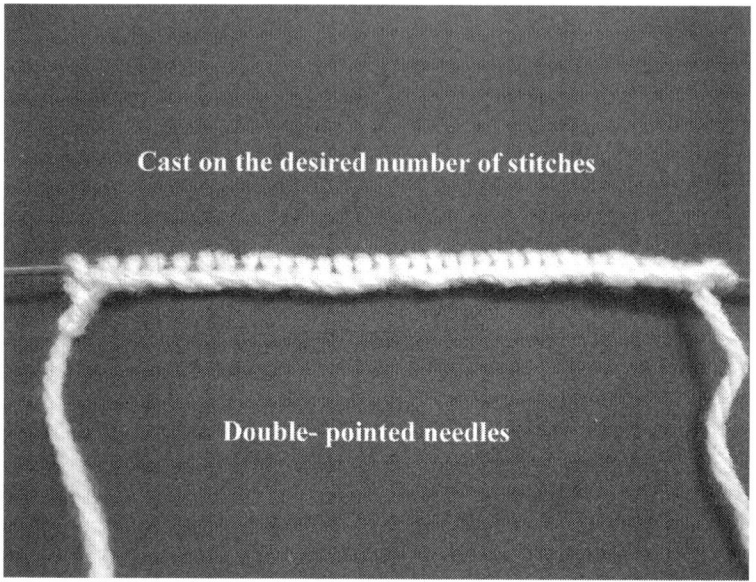

Divide the number of stitches into 4 even sections, one section for each of 4 needles.

For example, if you have 36 stitches, put 9 stitches onto each needle. Start with 36 stitches on one needle.

36 stitches divided by 4 = 9 stitches per needle.

Steps 1 and 2: Slide half of the stitches onto your second needle.

Now you have 18 stitches on each of two needles.

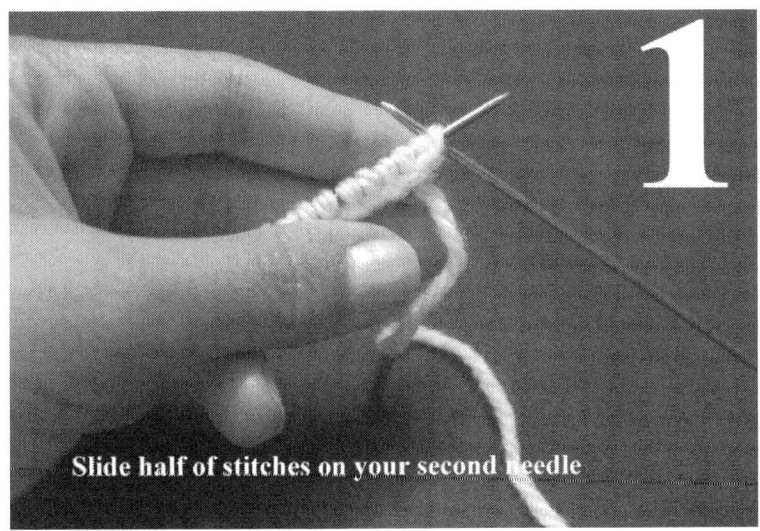

Slide half of stitches on your second needle

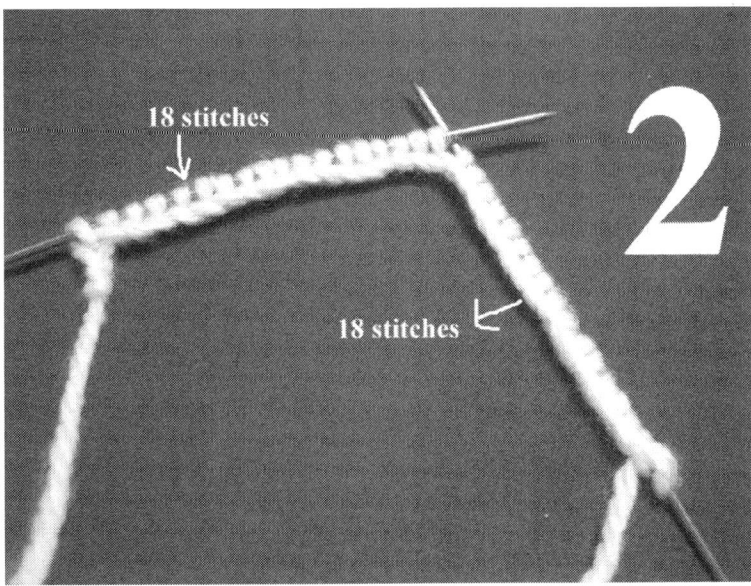

18 stitches

18 stitches

Steps 3 and 4: Slide half of the stitches off the second needle onto the third needle so now you have 9 stitches on the second and 9 on the third needle.

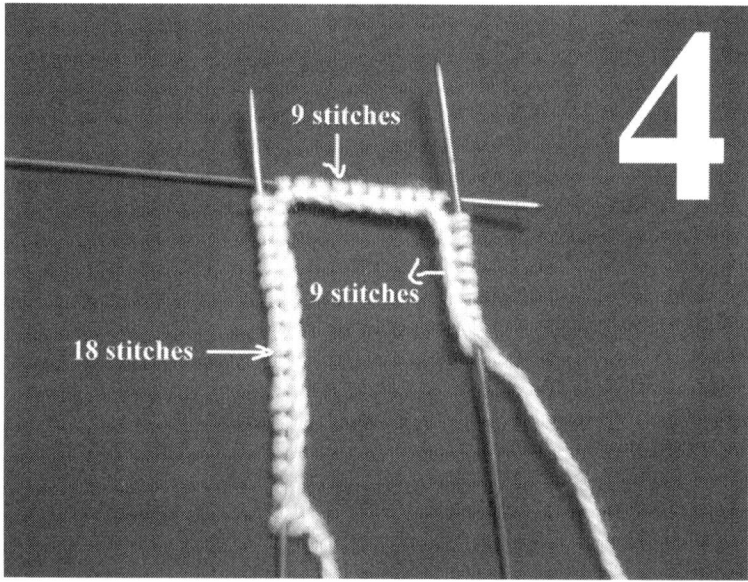

Steps 5 and 6: Slide half of the stitches off the first needle onto the fourth needle so now each of four needles has 9 stitches apiece.

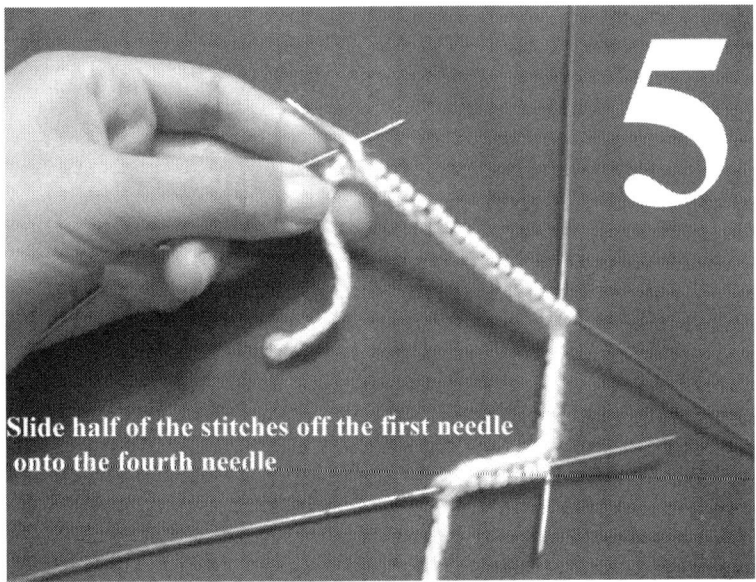

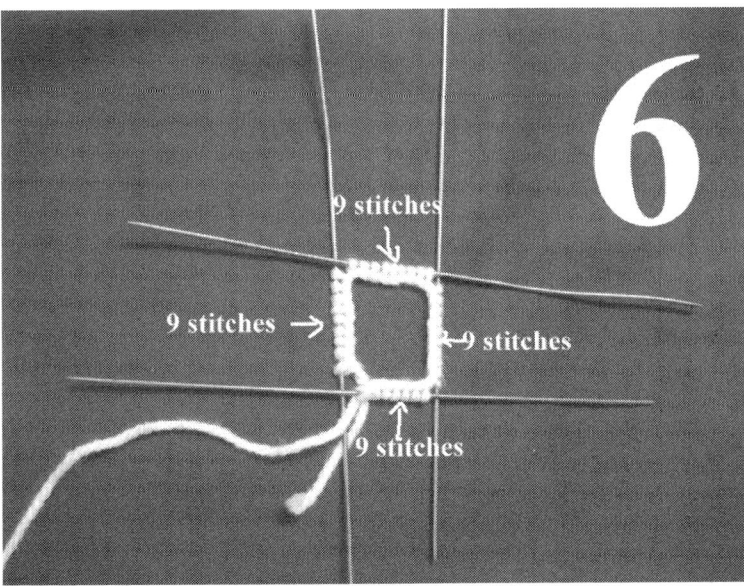

Step 7: Add a stitch marker between the last 2 stitches on the last needle to mark the end of each round.

Add a stitch marker between the last 2 stitches on the last needle to mark the end of each round

Step 8: Join the round by holding the needle with the working yarn by your right hand.

Hold the needle with the working yarn by your right hand.

Step 9: Insert your fifth needle into the first stitch.

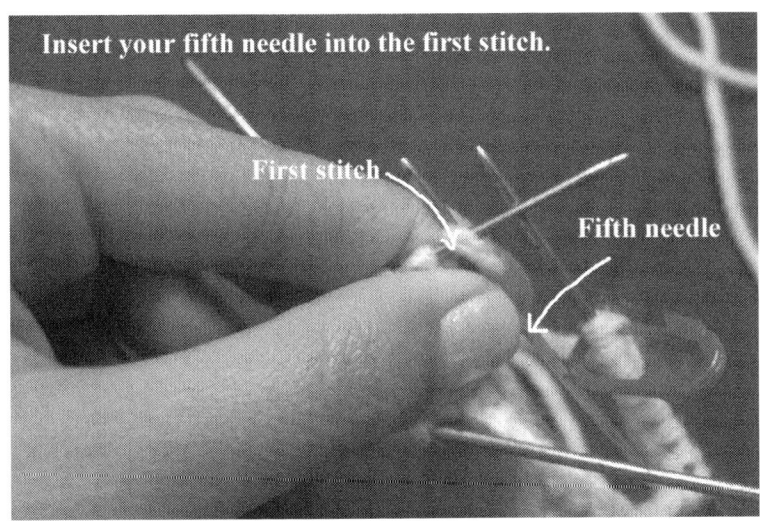

Step 10: Wrap the working yarn around your right-hand needle (the fifth needle).

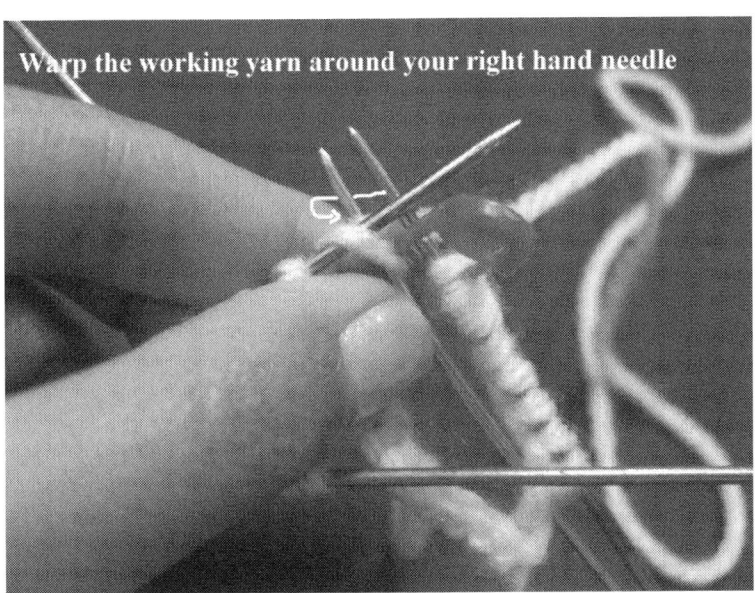

Step 11: Knit the stitch like normal by pulling the yarn through the stitch. Slide the stitch off your left needle. Make sure to tighten the yarn to maintain a square shape.

Step 12: Continue knitting by the same way you do on a regular needle until you have finished knitting all the stitches off the first needle.

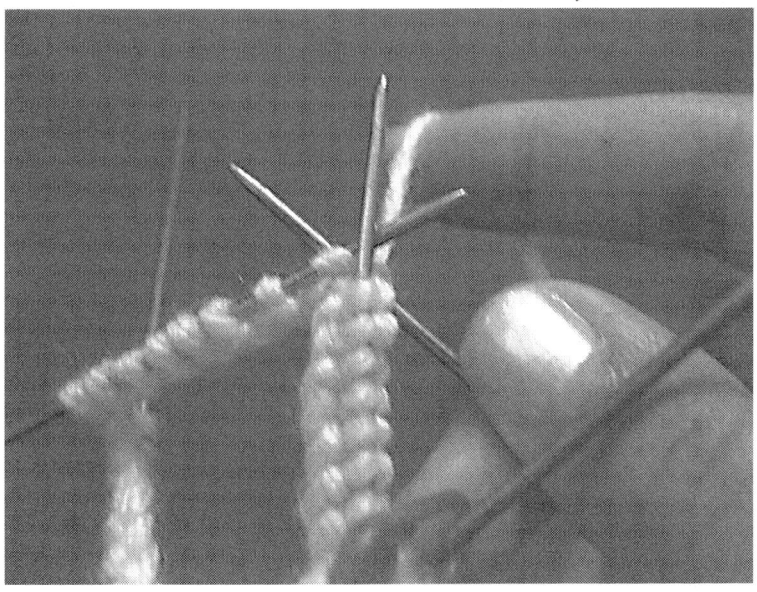

Knit the next set of stitches with a new empty needle.

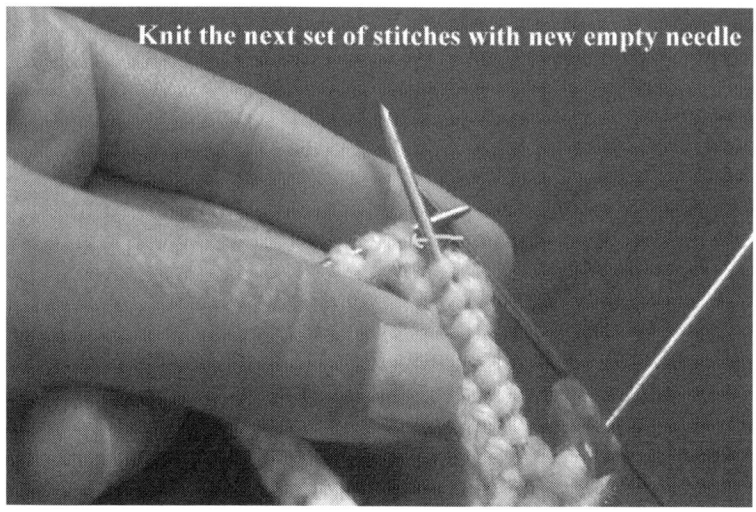

Continue knitting in this manner and make sure to tighten the yarn in each corner of the square until you reach the stitch marker.

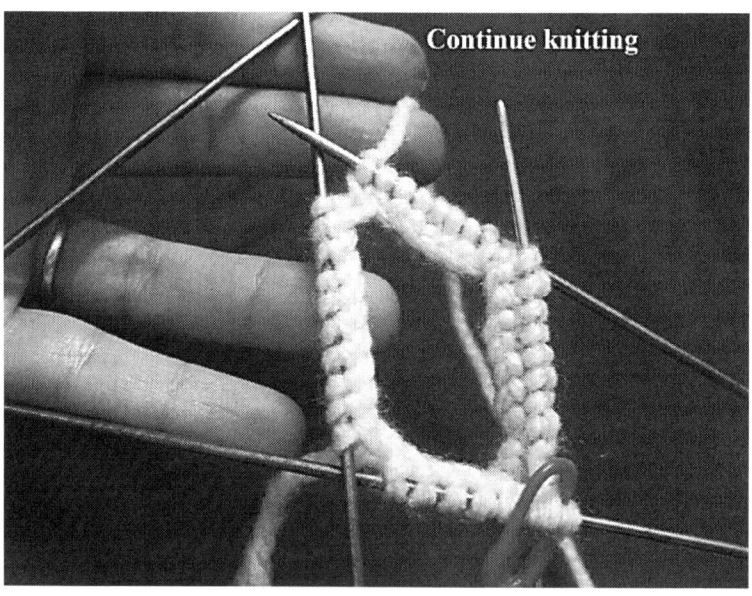

Step 13: Slip the stitch marker on your right needle and knit the last stitch. That completes the first round.

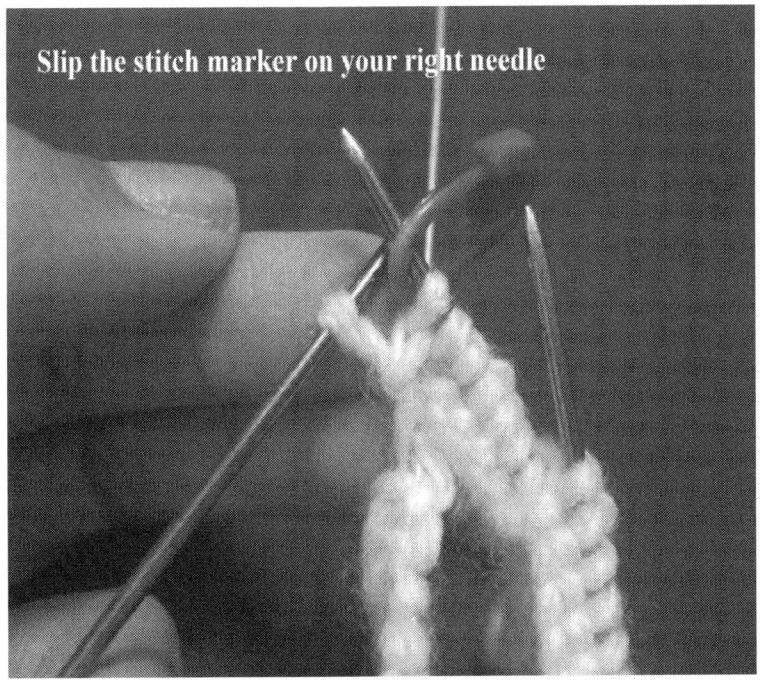

knit the last stitch

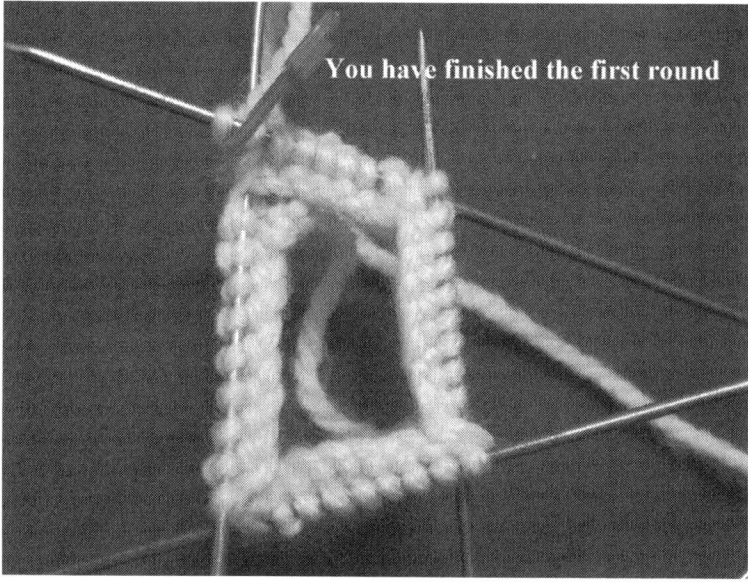

You have finished the first round

Start knitting the second round in the same way until you reach the desired length.

How to Increase in Knitting

There are four main methods to do increases while knitting.

We will examine each of them in depth.

The methods are make one (M1), yarn over (YO), knit front back (KFB), and adding stitches at the beginning.

Make One (M1)

The first method is known as M1. M1 stands for "make or increase one."

There are two types: M1 L (left) and M1 R (right). This method is used to add stitches between stitches.

This method is not utilized to add stitches at the start or end of rows.

First, we will examine the M1 R method.

M1 R (make one, right)

Step 1: Insert your left needle from the front to the back underneath the bar and in between two stitches.

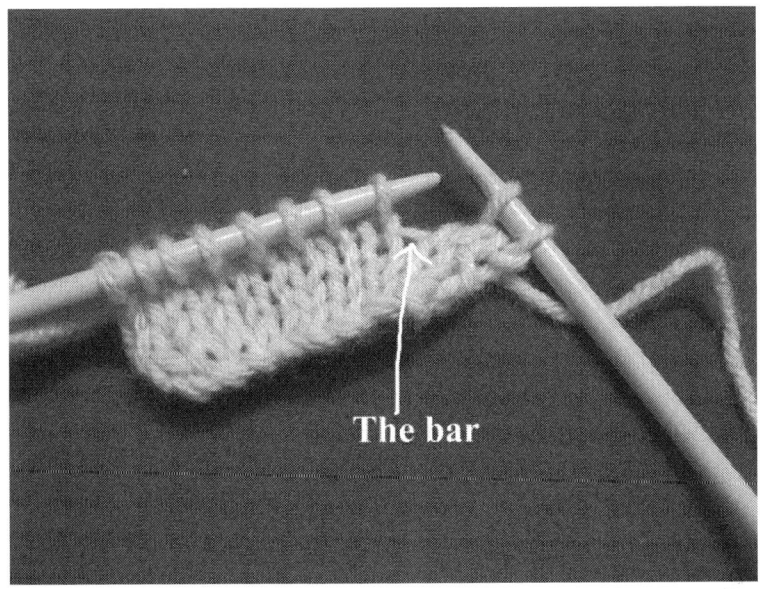

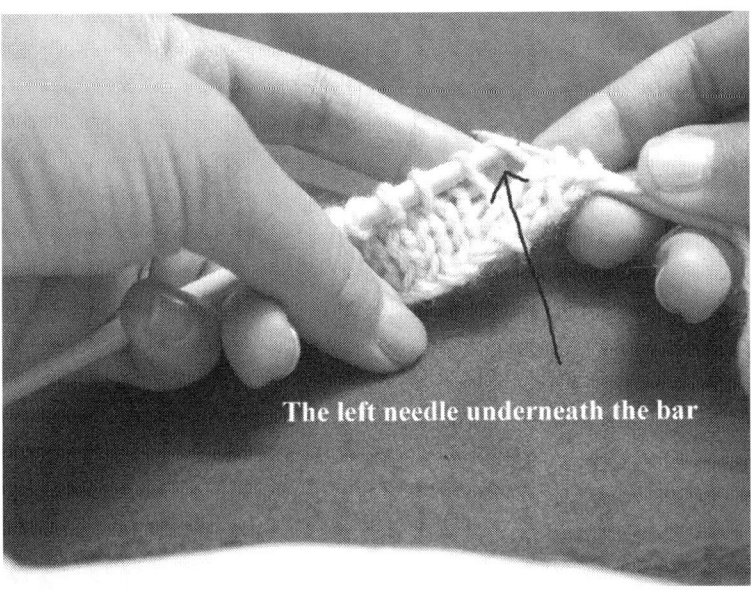

Step 2: Knit through the back of this loop to create a new stitch.

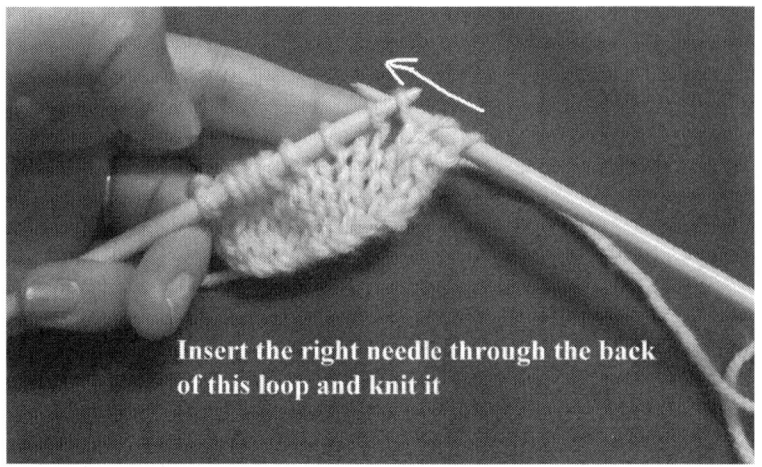

Insert the right needle through the back of this loop and knit it

The second M1 method is M1 L. We will look at this method next.

M1 L (make one, left)

Insert your left needle from the back to the front underneath the bar and in between two stitches.

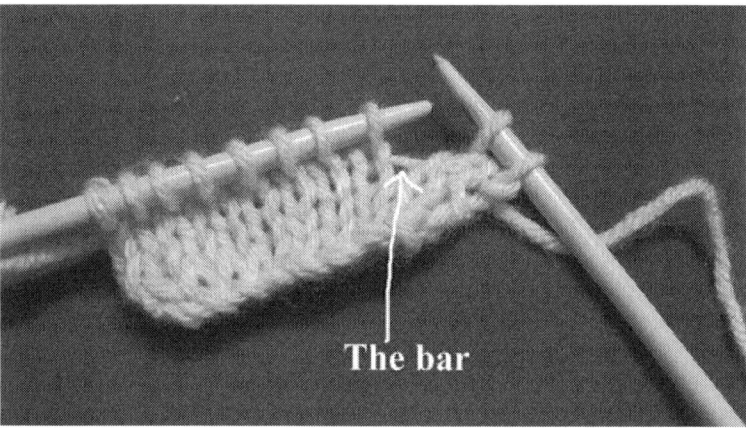

The bar

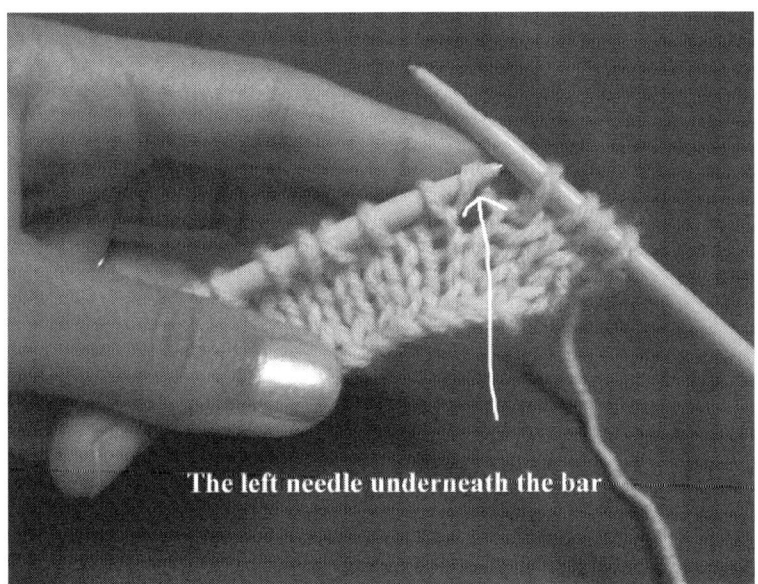

Knit through the front of this loop like a normal stitch.

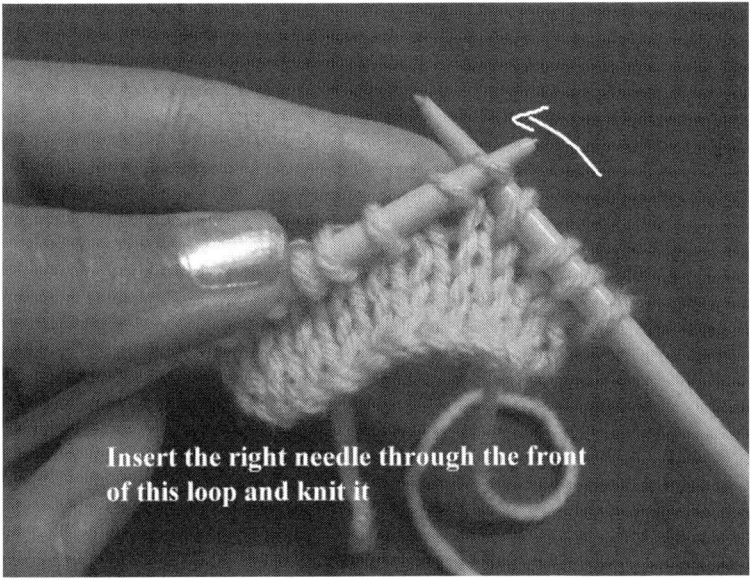

Yarn Over (YO)

The second method to increase stitches is known as YO. "YO" stands for "yarn over." This method is similar to M1 as it is also used to add stitches between stitches.

This method cannot be used to add stitches at the beginning of the row or at the end of the row. This method creates a large hole and is commonly used in lace stitches.

To make YO follow these steps.

Step 1: Knit the first stitch and then bring the working yarn to the front.

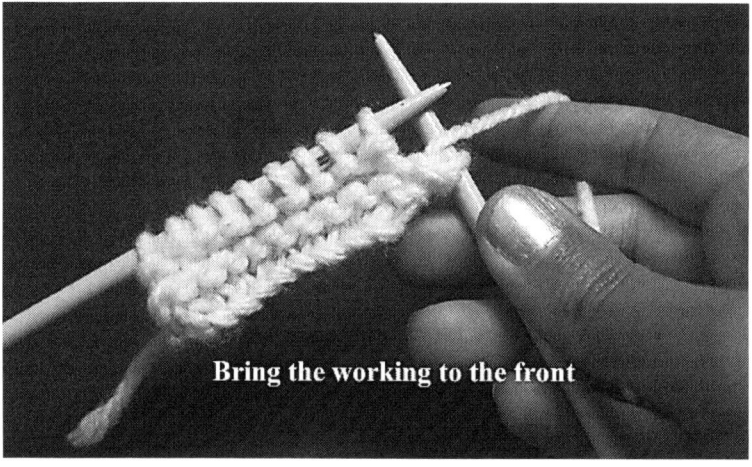
Bring the working to the front

Step 2: Wrap the working yarn across your left needle and return it to the back.

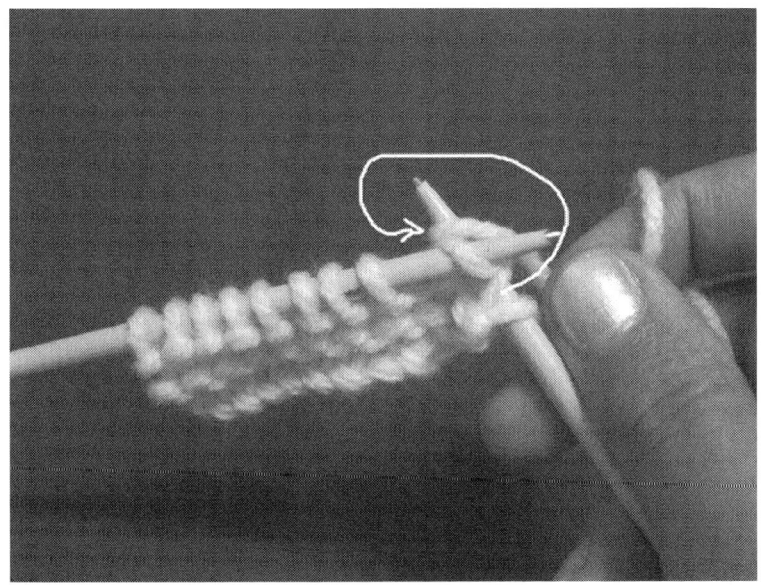

Knit the next stitch normally and continue knitting the row.

Step 3: In the next row, knit the stitches until you reach the YO stitch. Knit it as a normal stitch. Insert your right needle into the front of the YO and knit it.

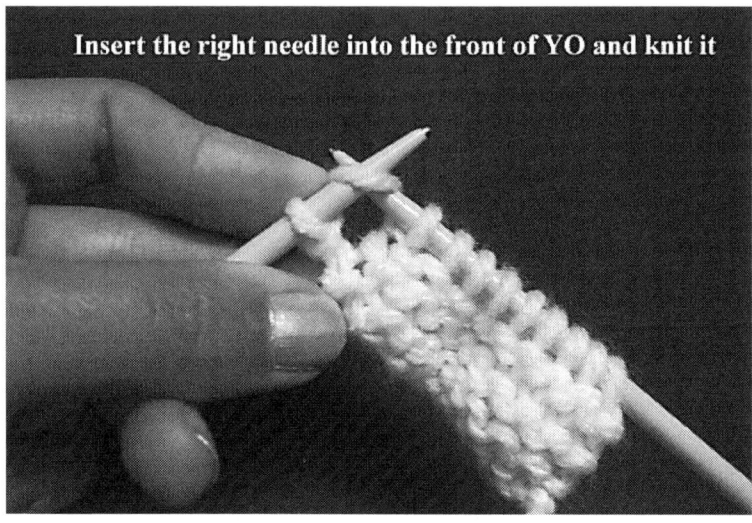

Using this approach creates a large hole. To avoid this, you can knit the decrease in an alternative way.

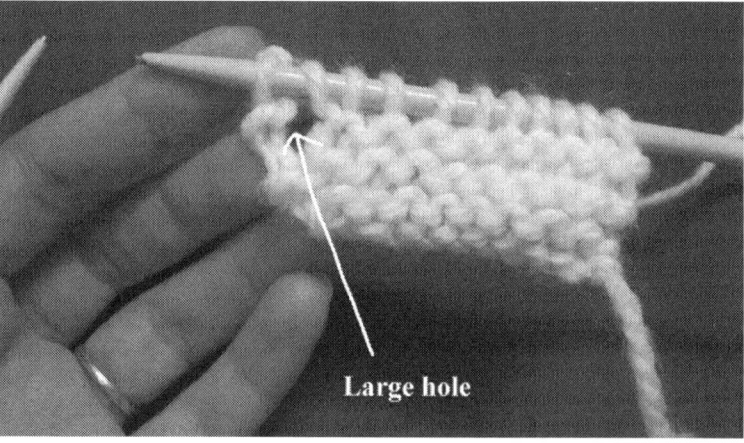

Insert your right needle into the back of the YO and then knit it normally.

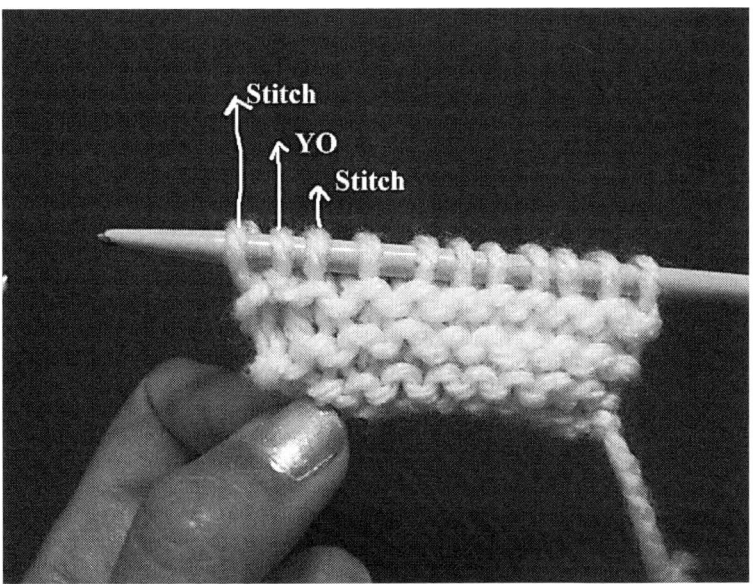

Knit Front Back (KFB)

The third method to increase in knitting is known as KFB. "KFB" stands for "knit front and back."

Just like the previous methods, this method is used to add stitches between stitches. This method cannot be used to add stitches at the beginning of the row or at the end of the row.

Knit the first stitch. Insert your right needle into the second stitch and knit it like a normal stitch. Don't slip the stitch off your left needle. Let it hang out on your left needle.

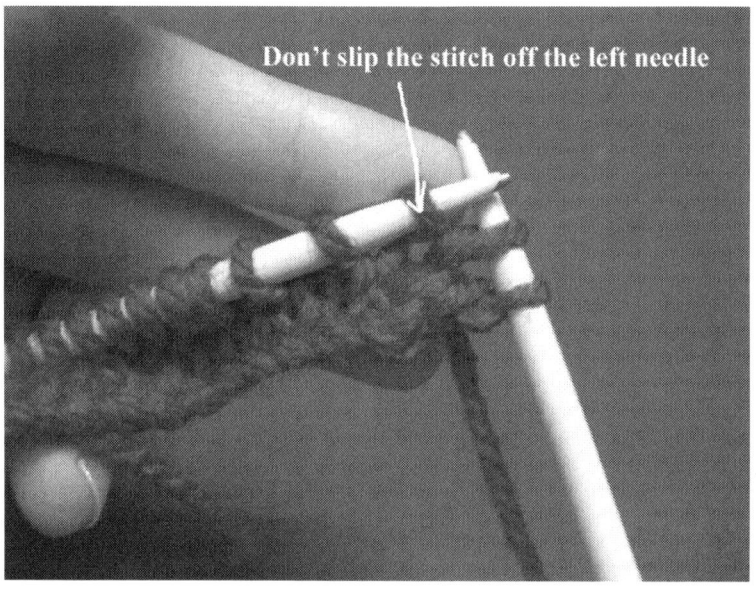

Insert the right needle into the same loop from the back. Knit a second stitch normally, resulting in two stitches from one.

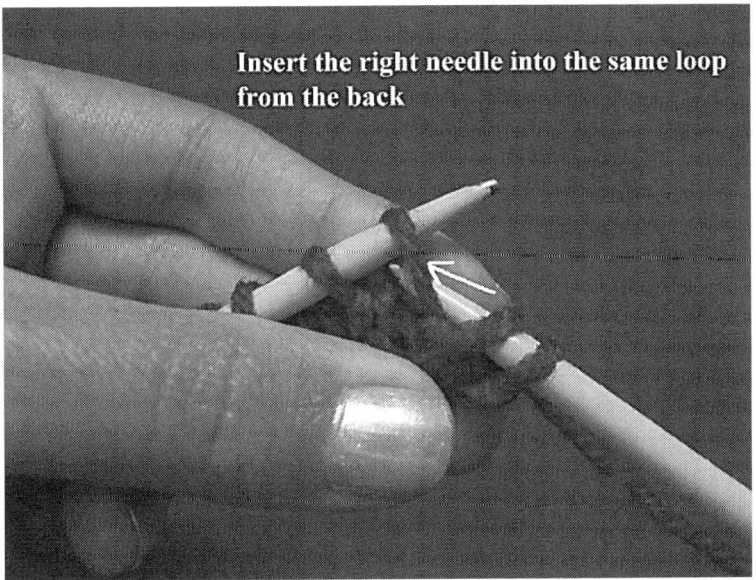

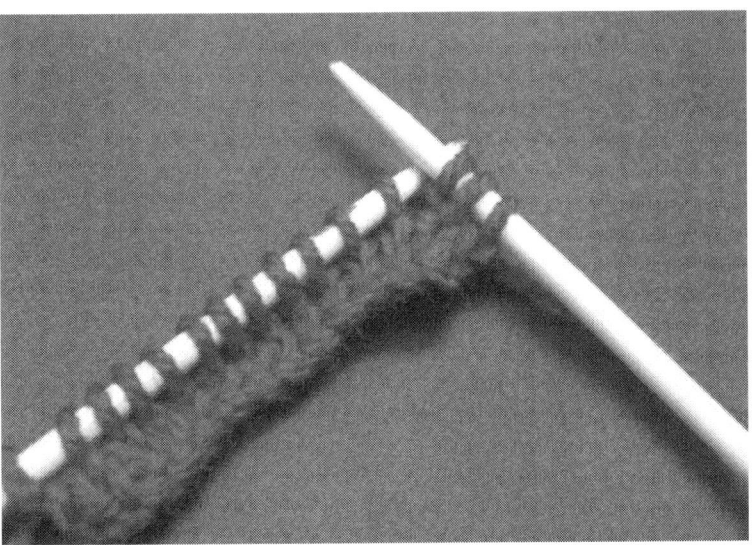

Add at the Beginning of a Row

Unlike the previously discussed methods, this fourth method to increase stitches is used to add more stitches at the beginning of the row.

At the beginning of the row, cast on the number of stitches you want to add by the cable cast-on method.

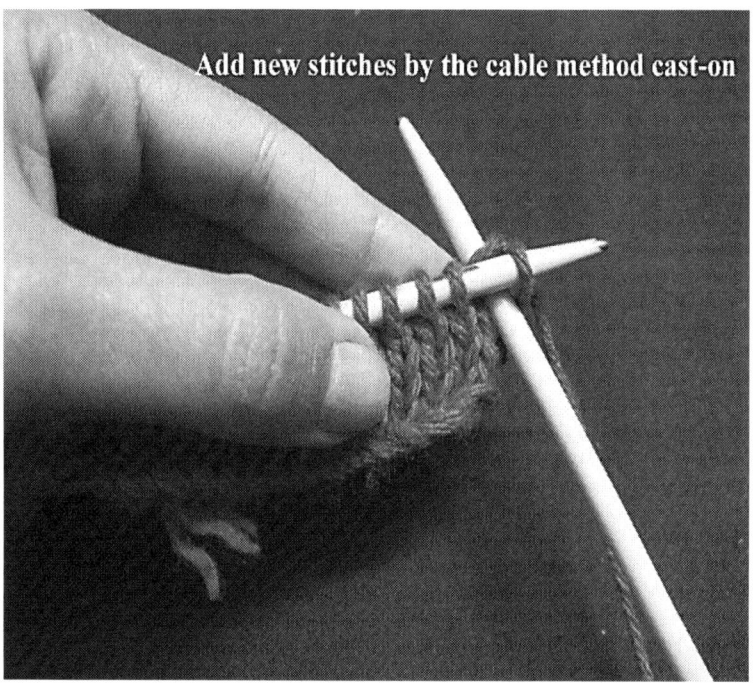

Knit all newly cast-on stitches.

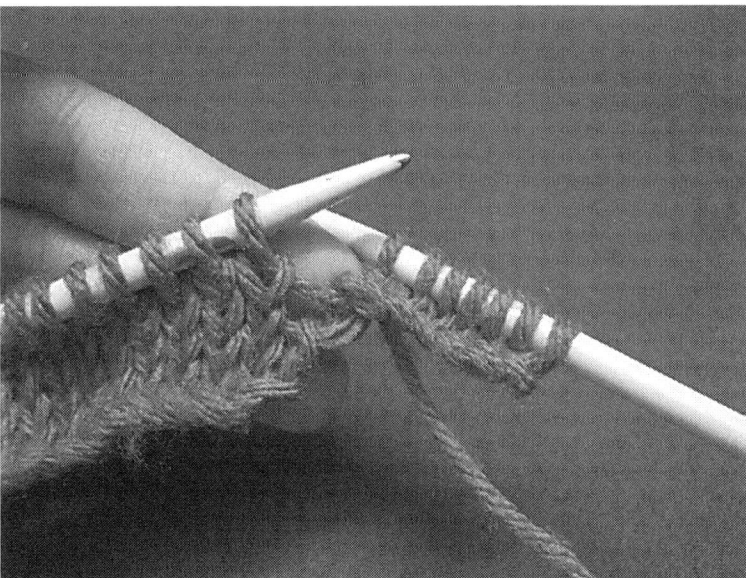

Continue knitting the row to incorporate the new stitches along with the old stitches.

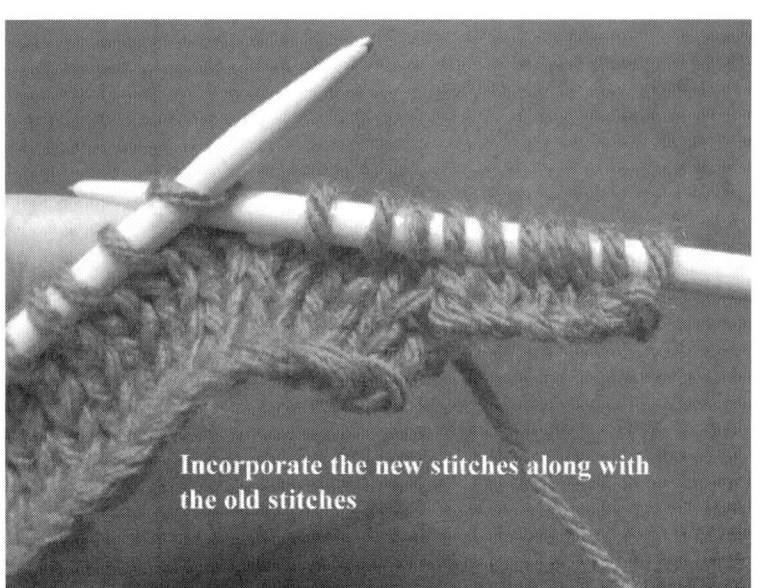

Incorporate the new stitches along with the old stitches

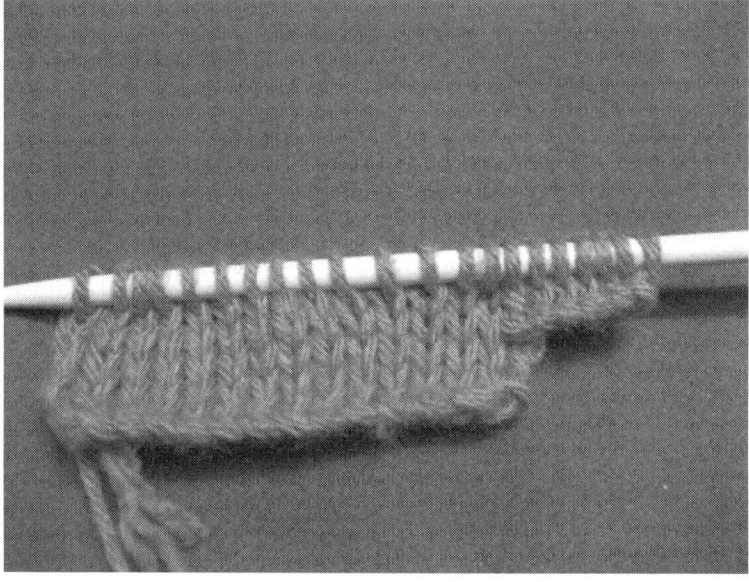

How to Decrease in Knitting

There are two methods to decrease stitches in knitting. These are knit 2 together (K2TOG) and slip, slip, and knit (SSK).

Knit Together (K2TOG)

The first method to decrease in knitting is known as K2TOG. "K2TOG" stands for "knit 2 together." This decreases slant to the right. This method can be used to decrease in the middle, beginning, or end.

Step 1: Instead of inserting your right needle into the first stitch, insert it into the second stitch on your left needle. Come up through the first stitch, so you have both stitches held.

Insert your right needle into the second stitch and then come up to the first

Knit them as one stitch normally. Wrap your yarn around and insert the needle through both loops. This results in one stitch made out of two stitches.

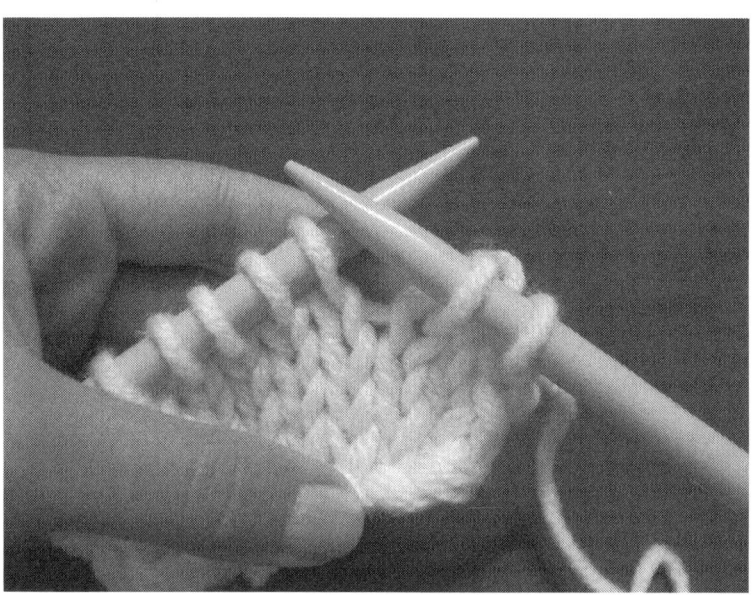

Slip, Slip, and Knit (SSK)

The second method to decrease in knitting is known as SSK. "SSK" stands for "slip, slip and knit." This decreases slant to the left.

Step 1: Insert your right needle into the stitch and slip it off the left needle onto the right needle.

Step 2: Slip the next stitch in the same manner.

Step 3: Insert your left needle into both front loops of these two stitches from left to right.

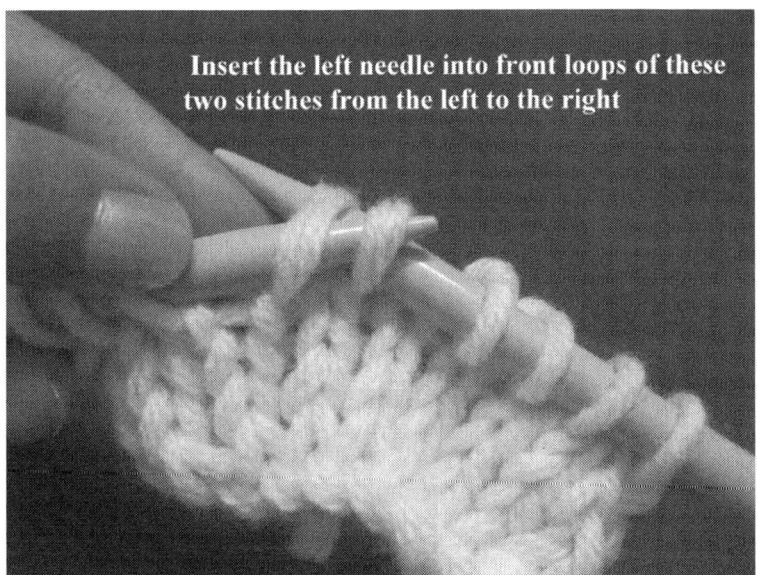

Wrap the yarn around your right needle. Knit the two slipped stitches together so the first stitch is on top and the last goes towards the left.

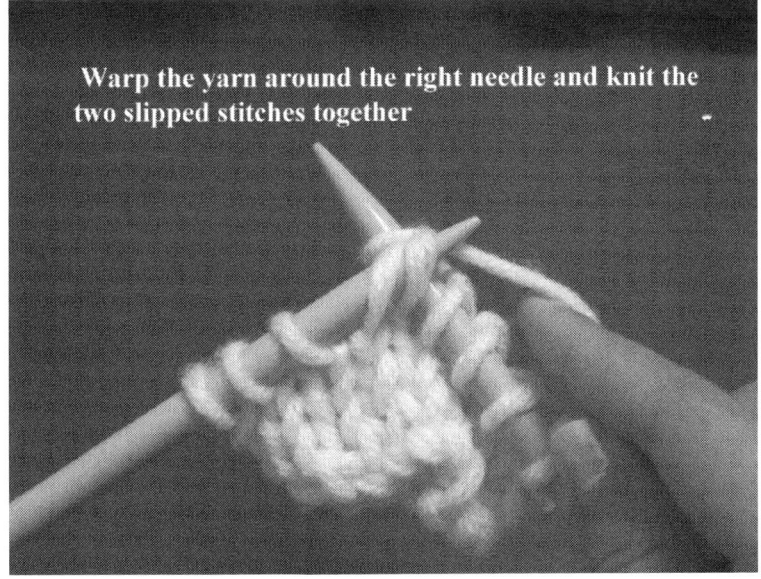

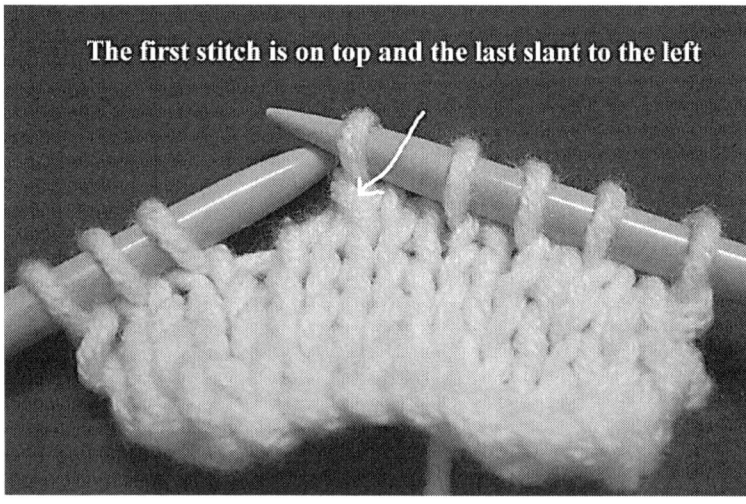

The first stitch is on top and the last slant to the left

How to Bind Off Knitted Stitches

To "bind off" means to end a column of stitches. It is the opposite of cast on. To do the basic knit bind off, follow the steps.

Step 1: Knit the first stitch as usual.

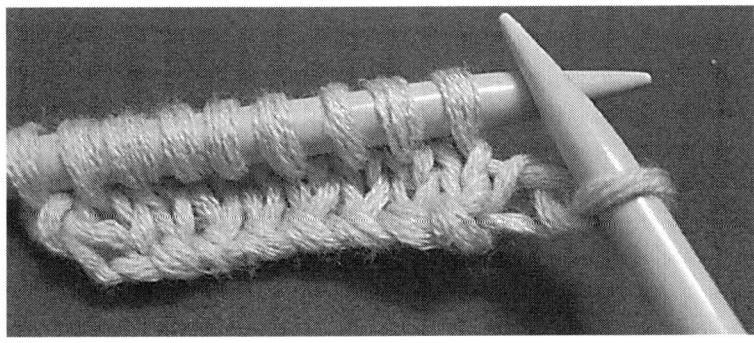

Step 2: Knit the second stitch in the same way.

Step 3: Using the left needle, pull the first stitch over the second one. Take it off the right needle.

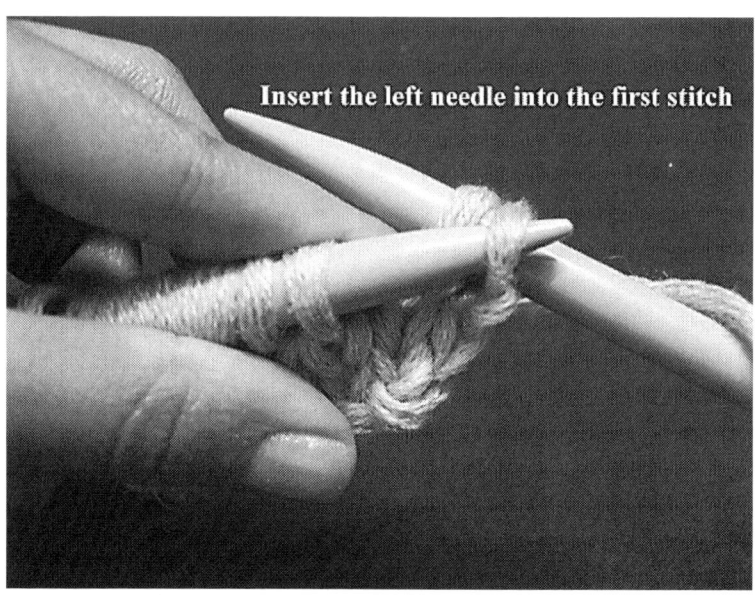

Step 4: Continue in the same manner. Knit the next stitch. Now you have two stitches placed on your right needle. Using the left needle pull the first stitch over the second one. Take it off the right needle.

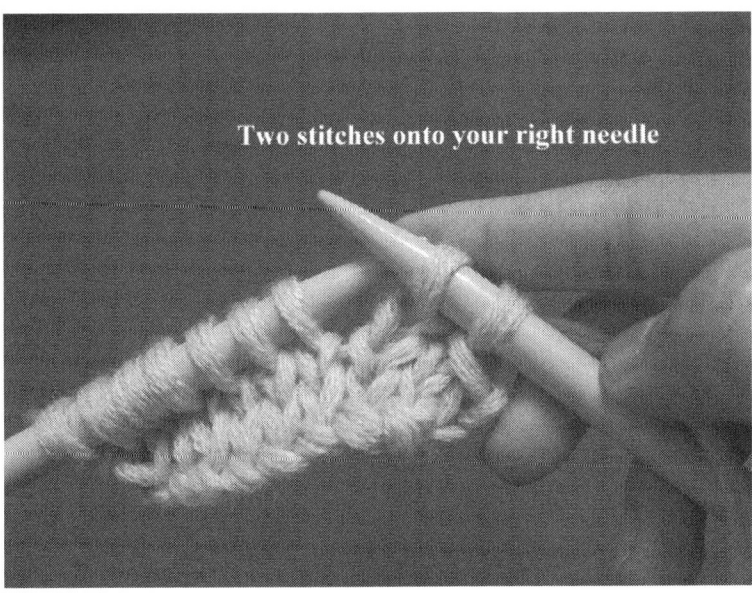

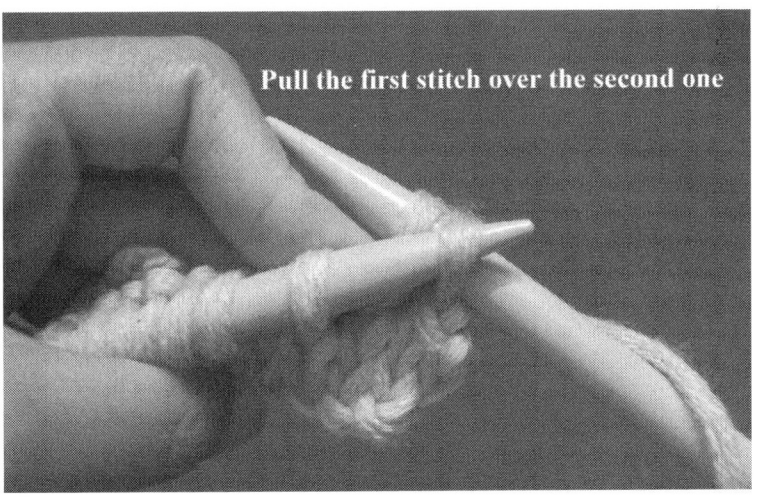

Step 5: Keep binding off until you reach the last stitch remaining on your right needle. Cut the working yarn and pull it through the last stitch.

More Common Stitches

The Garter Stitch

Now we will examine the most important stitch in knitting: the garter stitch. This means knitting in which all of the rows are knitted in knit stitch (K), rather than alternating with purl rows.

This type of stitching can be used for creating stretchy knitting. Knit all stitches in all rows with the knit stitch (K).

This stitch doesn't curl, so it is perfect for making scarfs and blankets.

Many different patterns feature the garter stitch.

Stockinette Stitch

The stockinette or stocking stitch is a way of stitching with having alternate rows of knit stitches and purl stitches, producing a fabric as for stockings.

The first row: knit all the stitches with the knit stitch (K).

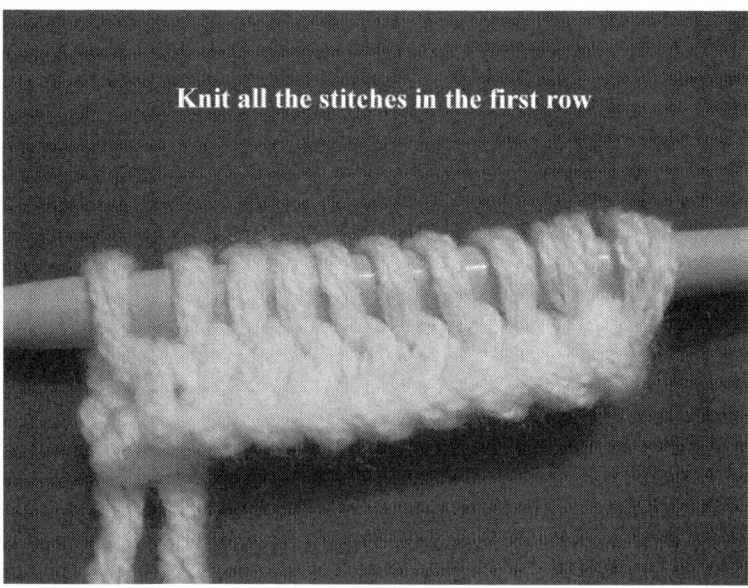

The second row: purl (P) all the stitches.

Continue in this manner, repeating the two rows from the first row.

Alternate each row between knit and purl stitches.

The third row and the rest of all odd rows do it as the first row with the knit stitch.

The fourth row and the rest of all even rows do it as the second row with a purl stitch.

Many patterns feature the stockinette stitch.

Stocking (stockinette) stitch has a right and wrong side. The right side is the smooth side (knit side), and the stitches look like small Vs.

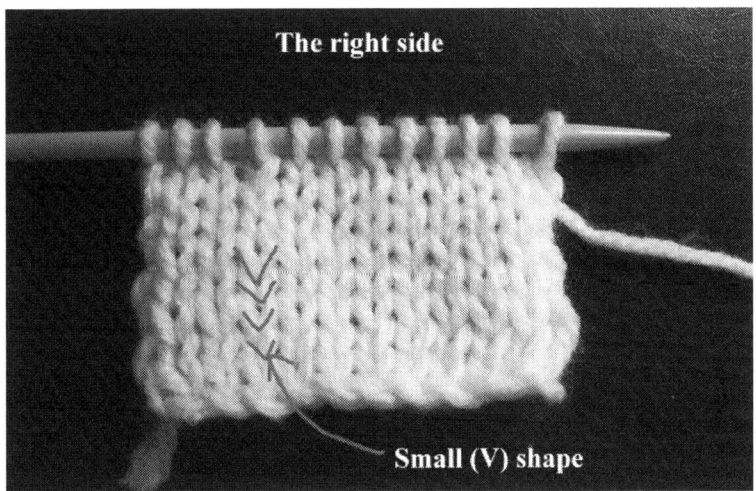

The wrong side is called the reverse side or purl side.

Rib Stitches

Single Rib Stitch

The rib stitch consists of columns of knit stitches alternating with columns of purl stitches. To make a ribbed pattern, you change from knit stitches to purl stitches within a row.

To make the basic elastic (single rib) stitch (1 x 1) follow these instructions.

Cast on a number of stitches that can be divided by 2.

Example: Cast on 12 stitches, 6 will be knit, 6 will be purl.

The first row: Knit 1, purl 1 (K1, P1) and repeat until the end of the row.

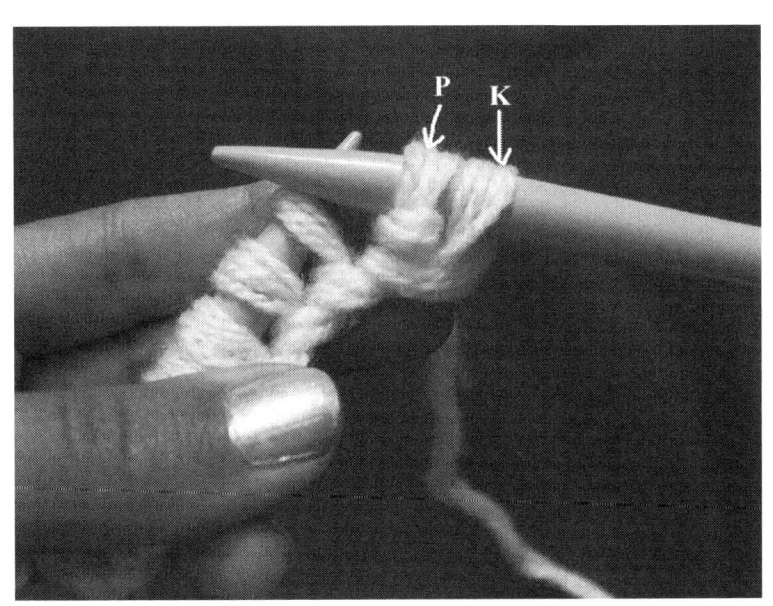

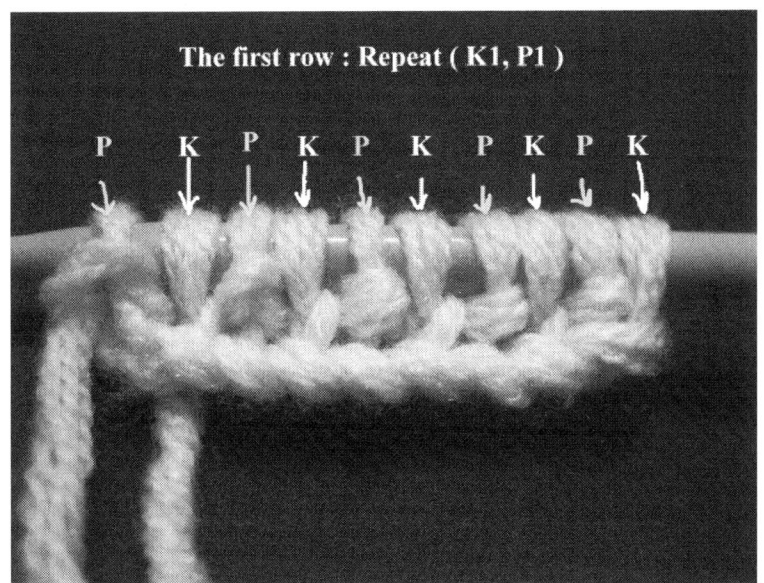

The second row: (K1, P1) repeat until the end of the row.

Continue in this manner, repeating the two rows from the first row.

The pattern is formed by alternating between knit and purl stitches to form vertical columns.

| Row 1 | K | P |
| Row 2 | K | P |

The rows look like this.

Dual Rib Stitch

The double rib stitch pattern creates a knit 2, purl 2 (K2, P2) pattern in the fabric.

To make a dual rib stitch (2x2), you first have to cast on a number of stitches that can be divided by 4.

The first row: (K2, P2), repeat until the end of the row.

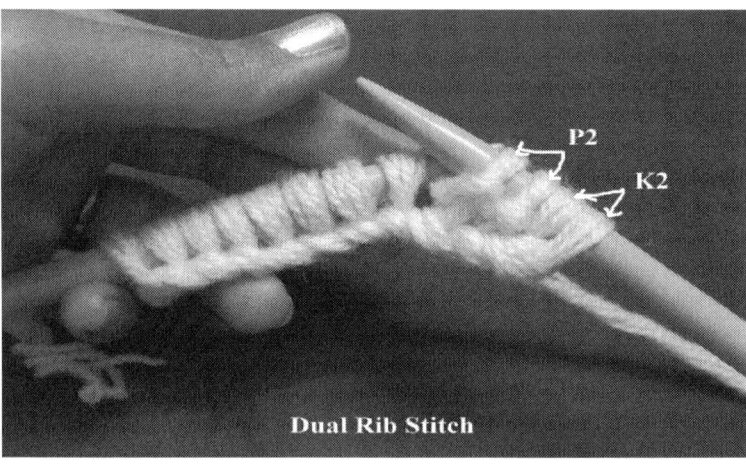

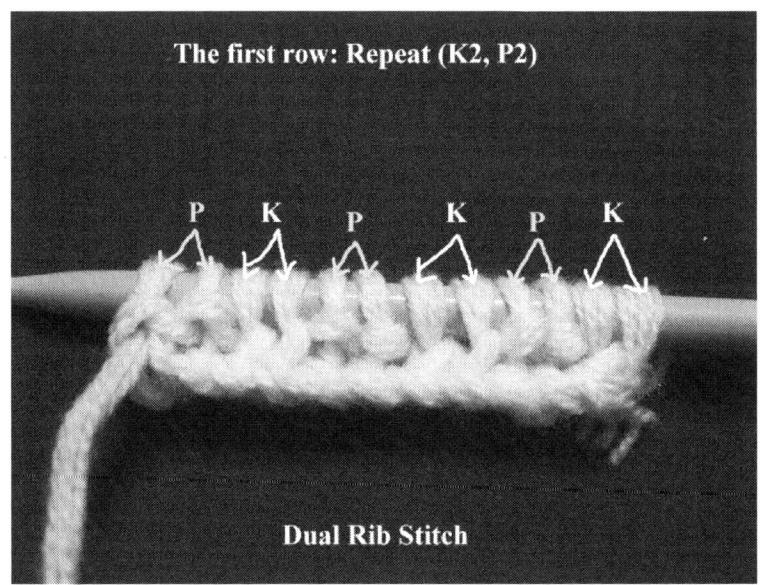

The second row: (K2, P2) repeat until the end of the row.

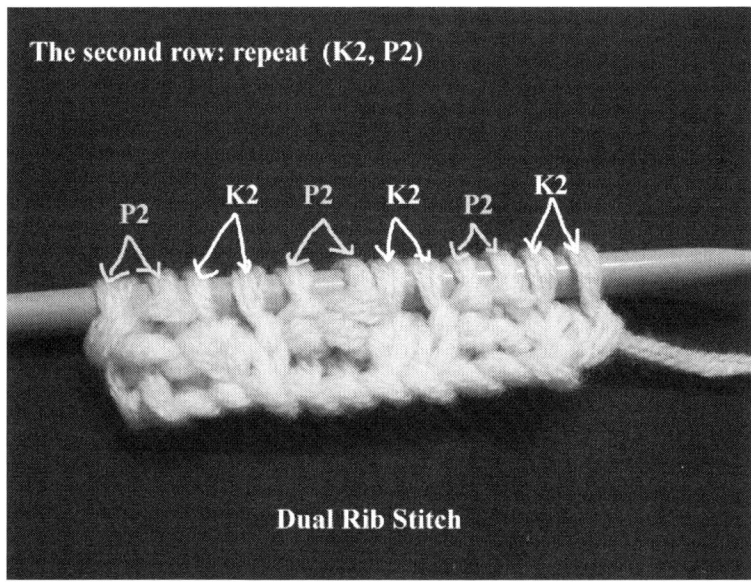

Repeat the 2 rows from the first row.

This is the pattern of the rows.

Row 1	K	K	P	P
Row 2	K	K	P	P

Two to One Rib Stitch

To make the two to one rib stitch (2x1), first cast on a number of stitches that can be divided by 3.

The first row: (K2, P1) repeat for the row.

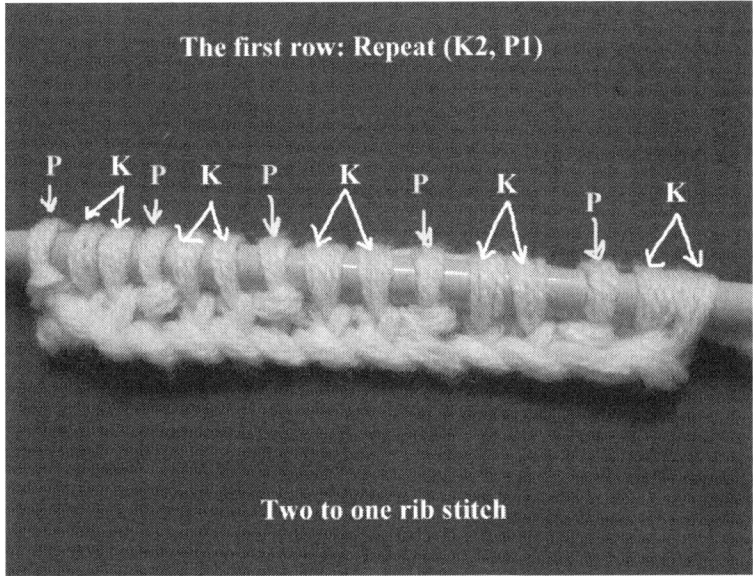

The second row: Switch the order (K1, P2)

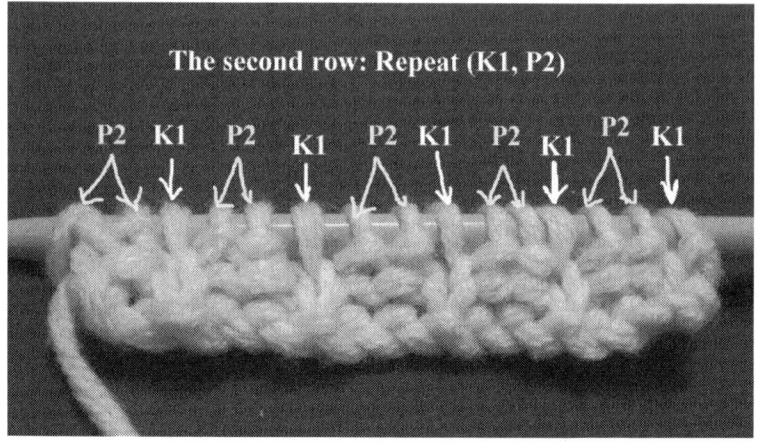

Do the rest of odd rows as the first row (K2, P1). Do the rest of even rows as the second row (K1, P2).

Shaped Stitches

Square Stitch (2x2)

Cast number of stitches that can be divided on 4.

The first row: (K4, P4) repeat for the row.

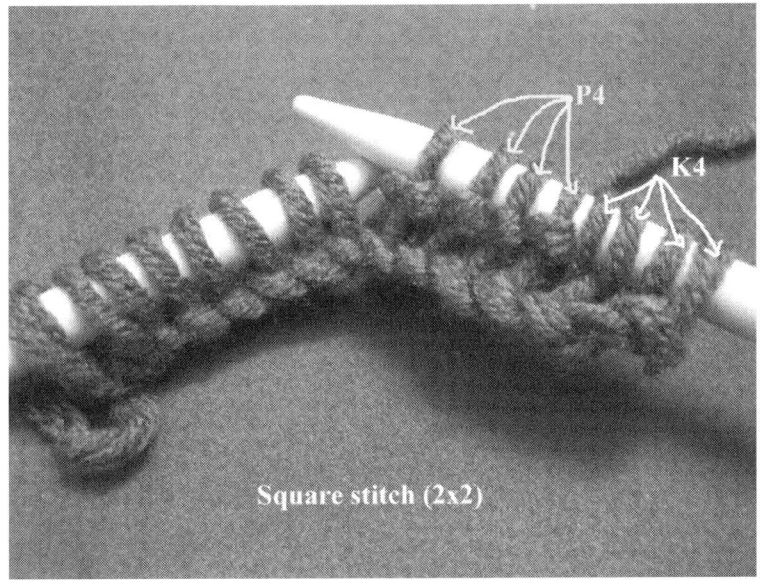

Square stitch (2x2)

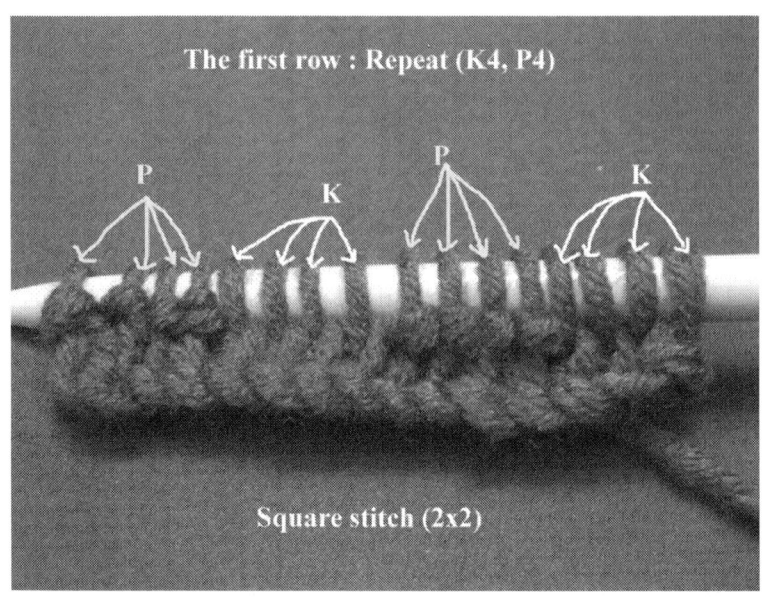

Rows 1-4: Repeat the first row until the fourth row

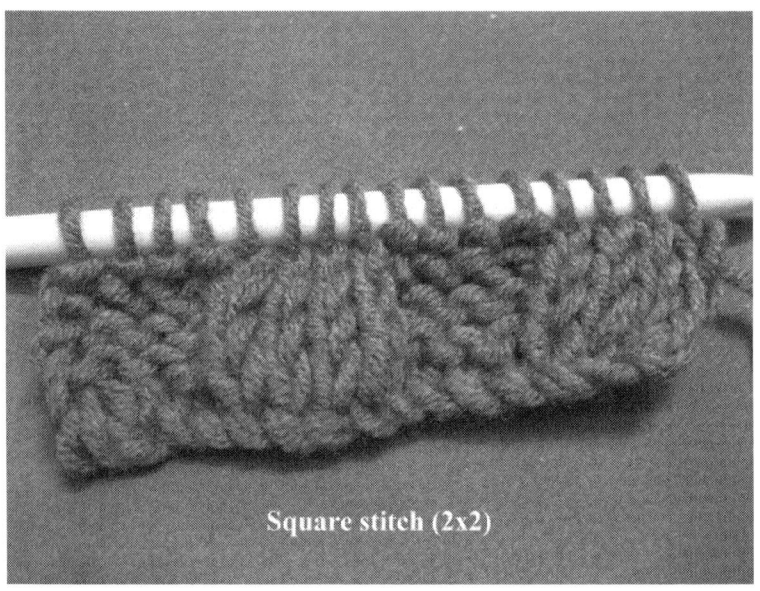

Row 5: (P4, K4) repeat until the end of the row.

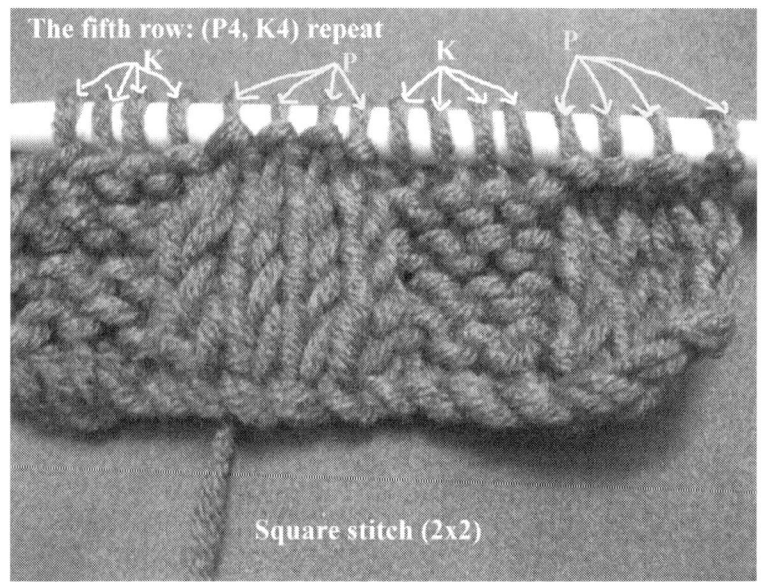

Repeat the fifth row until the eighth row.

Repeat the pattern of the first 4 rows, alternating every 4 rows, until you have achieved the desired length.

Rows 1-4 (K4, P4)

Rows 5-8 (P4, K4)

Rows 9-12 (K4, P4)

Rows 13-16 (P4, K4)

Rows 17-20 (K4, P4)

Repeat as needed.

Here is a chart to illustrate the rows

Row 1	K	K	K	K	P	P	P	P
Row 2	K	K	K	K	P	P	P	P
Row 3	K	K	K	K	P	P	P	P
Row 4	K	K	K	K	P	P	P	P
Row 5	P	P	P	P	K	K	K	K
Row 6	P	P	P	P	K	K	K	K
Row 7	P	P	P	P	K	K	K	K
Row 8	P	P	P	P	K	K	K	K

Horizontal Rectangle Stitch

First, cast on a number of stitches that can be divided by 10.

Rows 1-3: (K5, P5) repeat for the row.

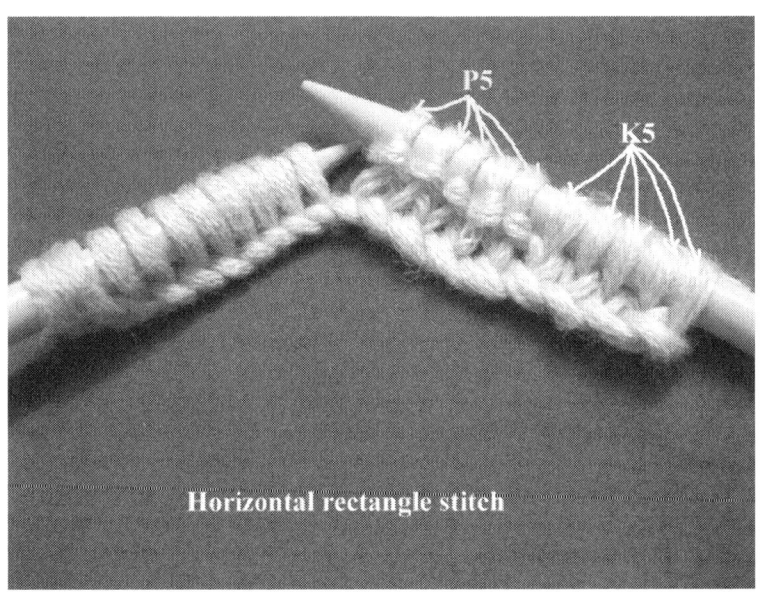

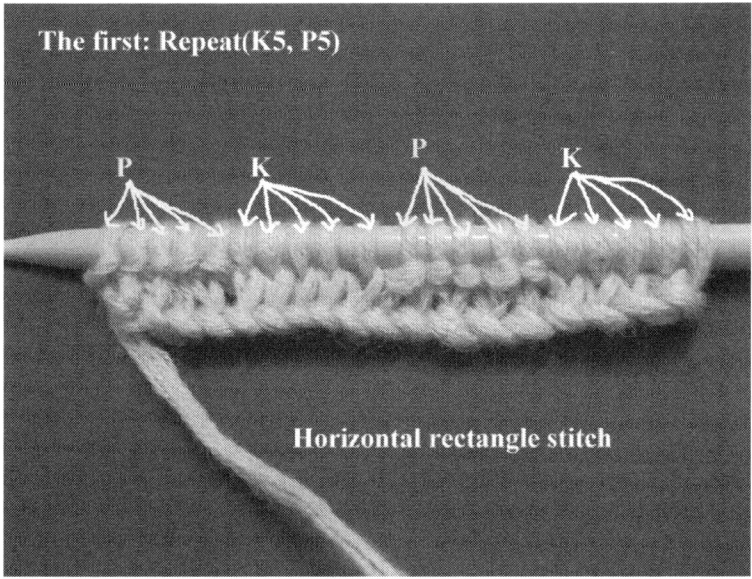

Do the second and the third row as the first row.

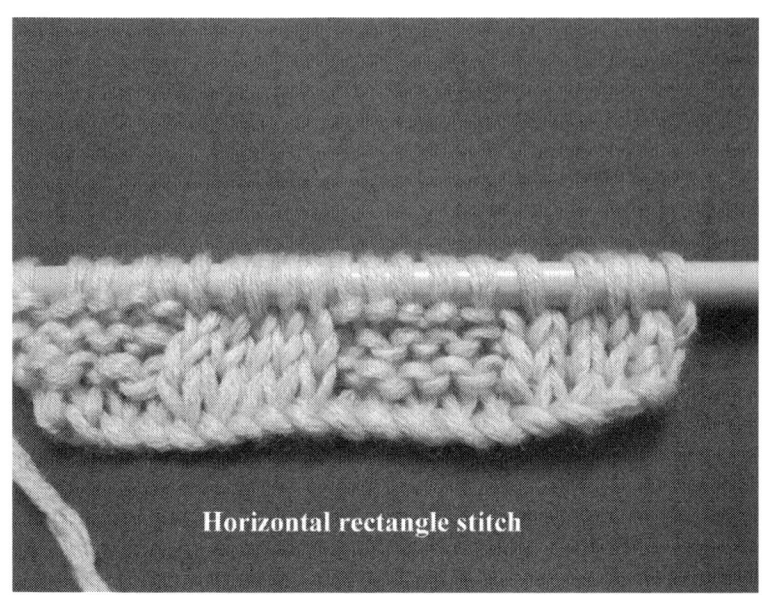

Horizontal rectangle stitch

Rows 4-6: (P5, K5) repeat until the end of the rows.

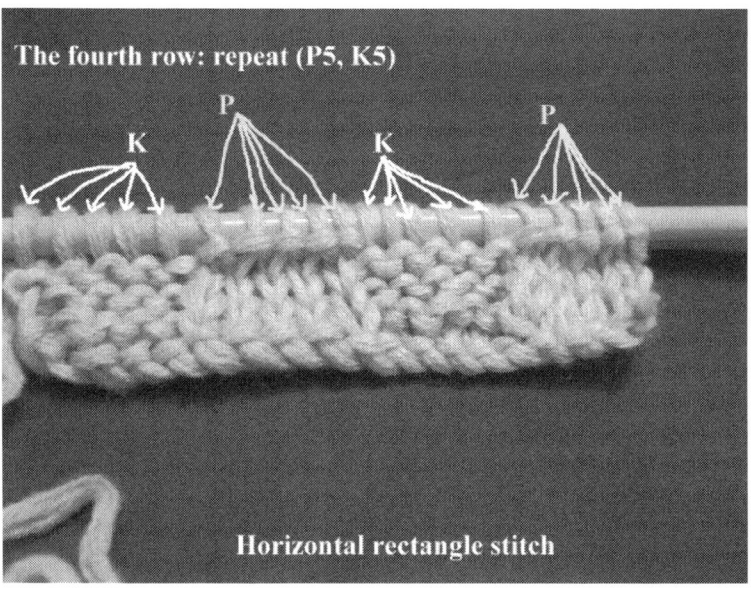

The fourth row: repeat (P5, K5)

Horizontal rectangle stitch

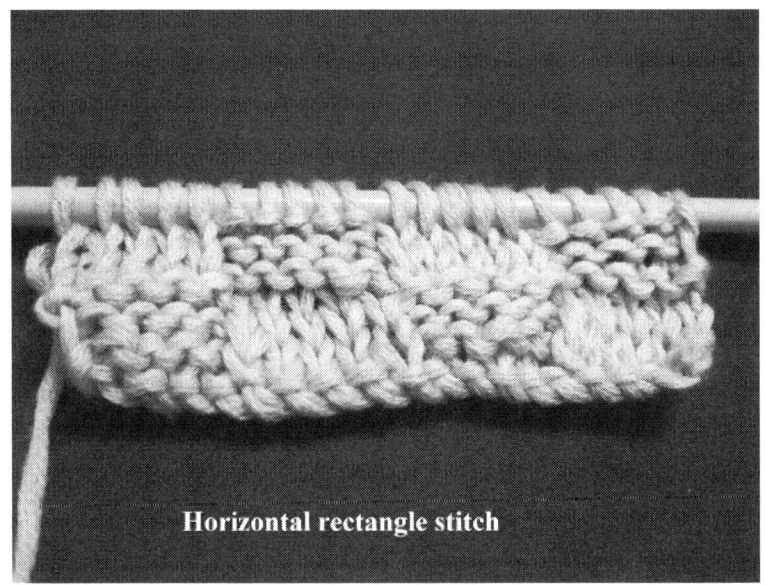

Horizontal rectangle stitch

Continue in this manner, repeating the six rows from the first row.

Horizontal rectangle stitch

Row 1	K	K	K	K	K	P	P	P	P	P
Row 2	K	K	K	K	K	P	P	P	P	P
Row 3	K	K	K	K	K	P	P	P	P	P
Row 4	P	P	P	P	P	K	K	K	K	K
Row 5	P	P	P	P	P	K	K	K	K	K
Row 6	P	P	P	P	P	K	K	K	K	K

Vertical Rectangle Stitch

First, cast on the number of stitches that can be divided by 6.

The first row: (K3, P3) repeat until the end of the row.

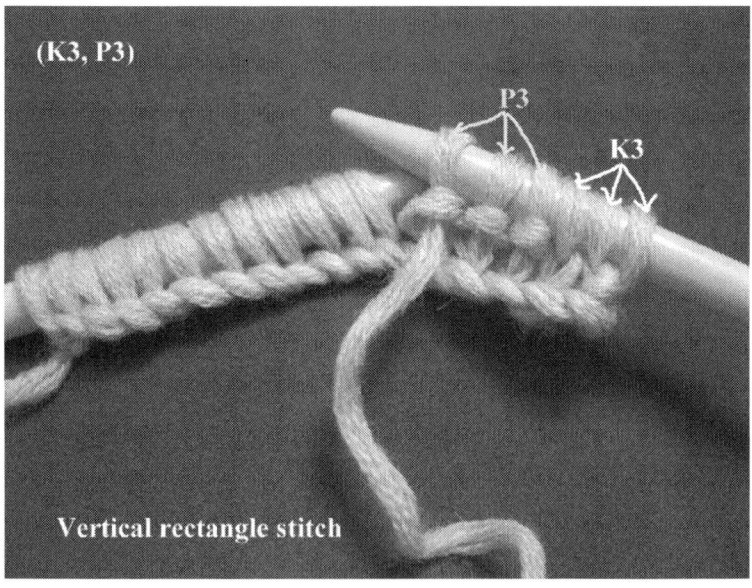

Vertical rectangle stitch

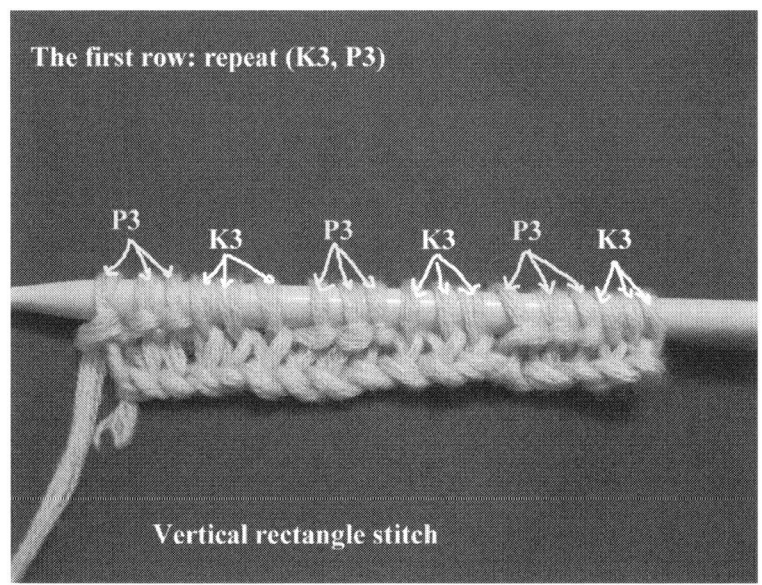

Row 2 and all even rows: purl (P) all the stitches.

Odd Rows: The third, fifth, seventh, ninth, and eleventh rows, do the same as the first row (K3, P3).

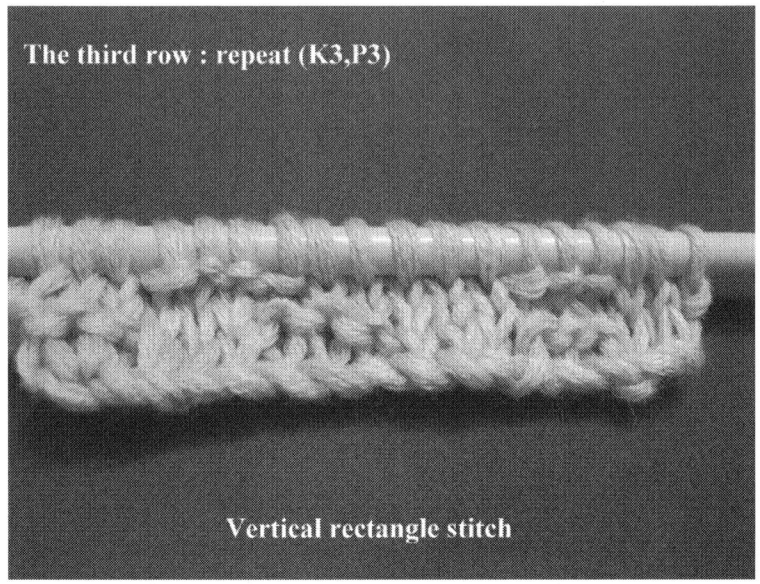

Row 12: Purl (P) all the stitches.

Rows 13, 15, 17, 19 and 21: (P3, K3) repeat until the end of the rows.

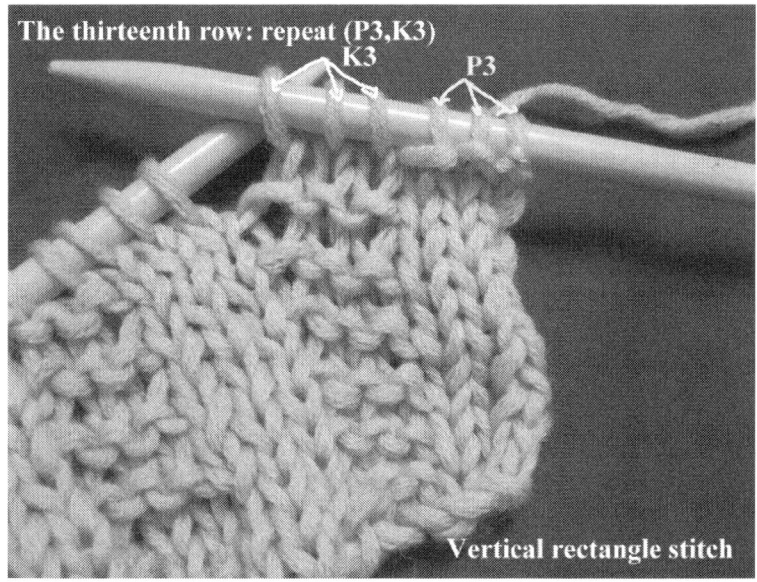

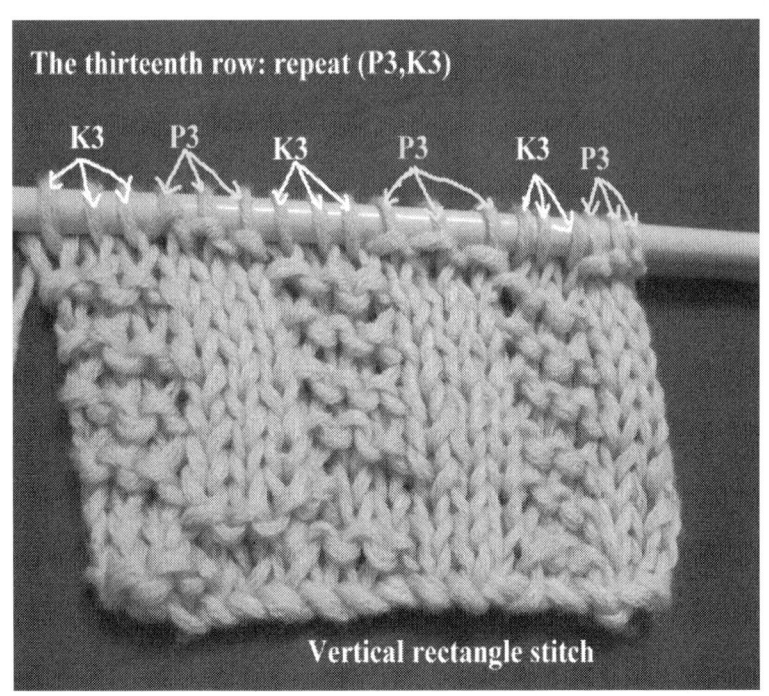

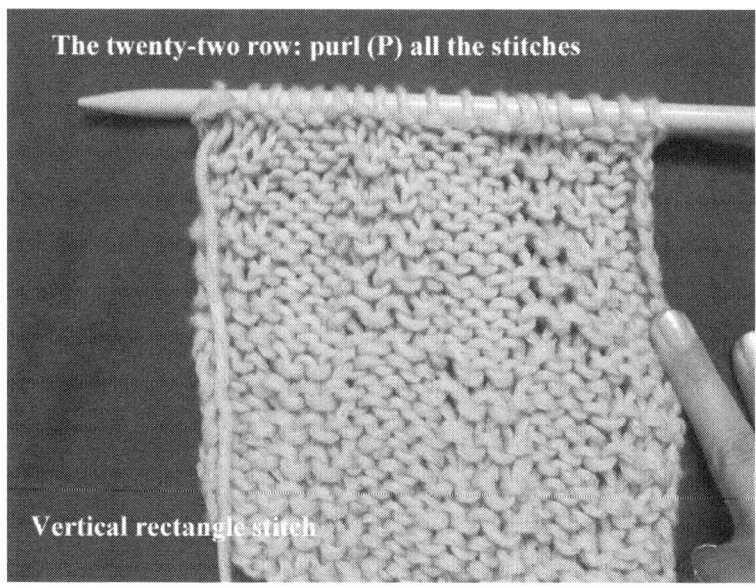

Continue this pattern, repeating the twenty-two rows from the first row.

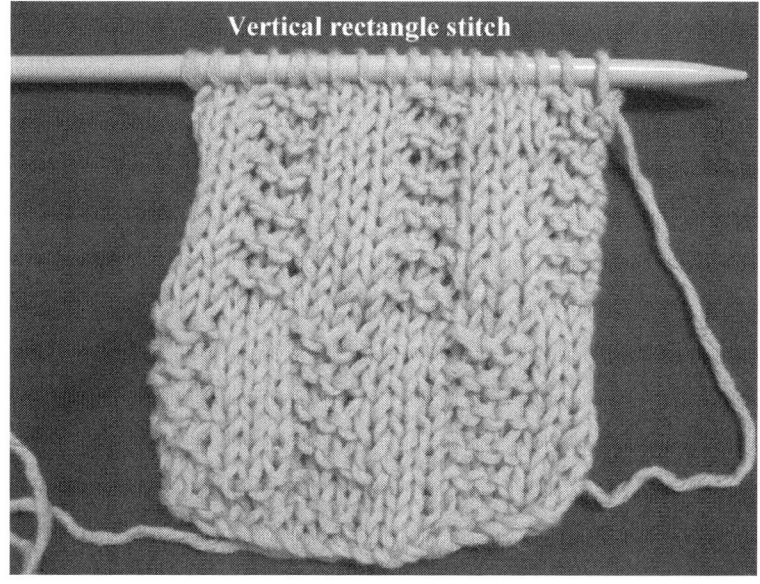

Row 1	K	K	K	P	P	P
Row 2	P	P	P	P	P	P
Row 3	K	K	K	P	P	P
Row 4	P	P	P	P	P	P
Row 5	K	K	K	P	P	P
Row 6	P	P	P	P	P	P
Row 7	K	K	K	P	P	P
Row 8	P	P	P	P	P	P
Row 9	K	K	K	P	P	P
Row 10	P	P	P	P	P	P
Row 11	K	K	K	P	P	P
Row 12	P	P	P	P	P	P
Row 13	K	K	K	P	P	P
Row 14	P	P	P	P	P	P
Row 15	K	K	K	P	P	P
Row 16	P	P	P	P	P	P
Row 17	K	K	K	P	P	P
Row 18	P	P	P	P	P	P
Row 19	K	K	K	P	P	P
Row 20	P	P	P	P	P	P
Row 21	K	K	K	P	P	P

Triangle stitch

To start, cast on a number of stitches that can be divided by 6. **Row 1:** Purl (P) all the stitches.

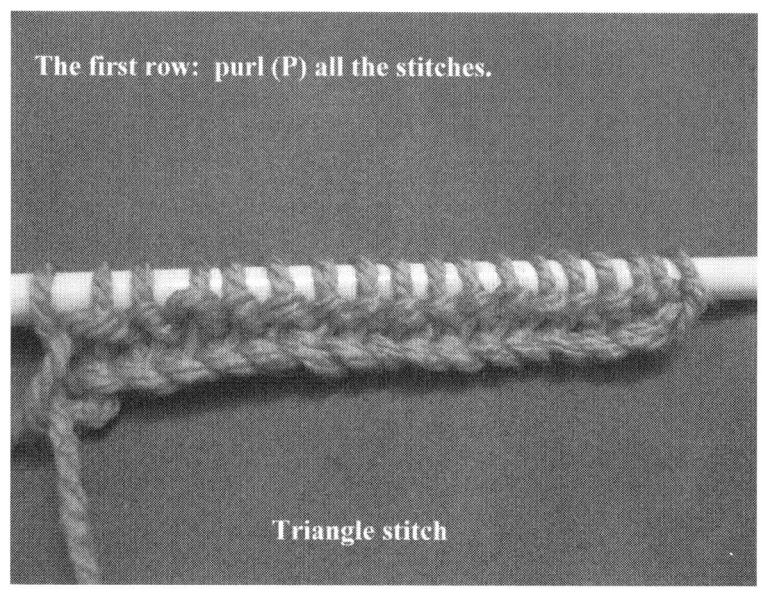

Row 2: (K5, P1) repeat until the end of the row.

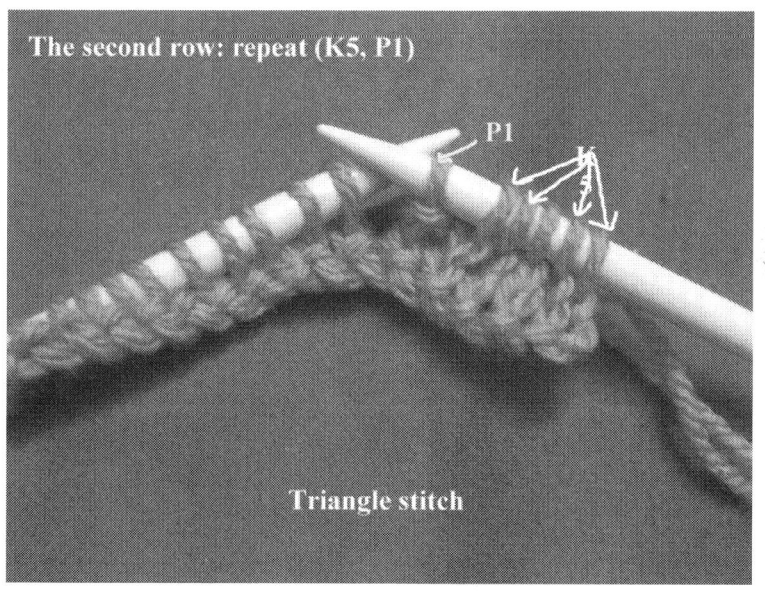

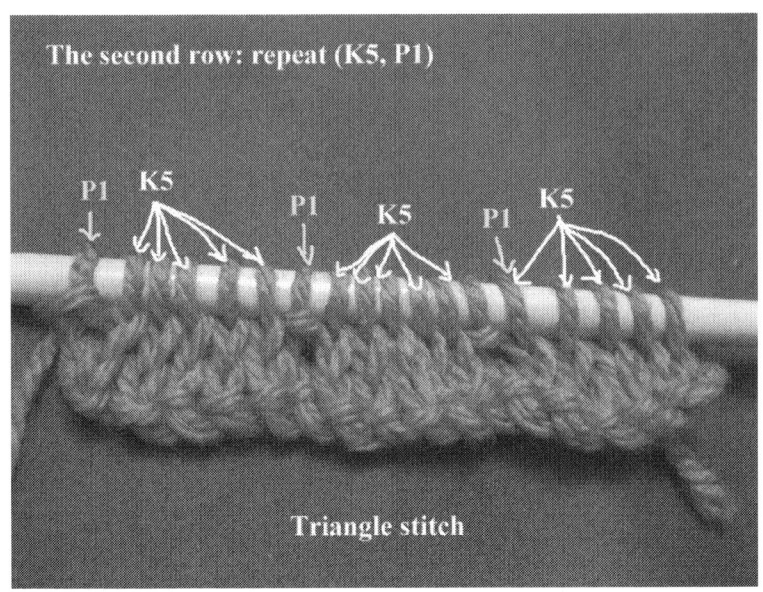

Row 3: (K1, P4, K1) repeat to the end of the row.

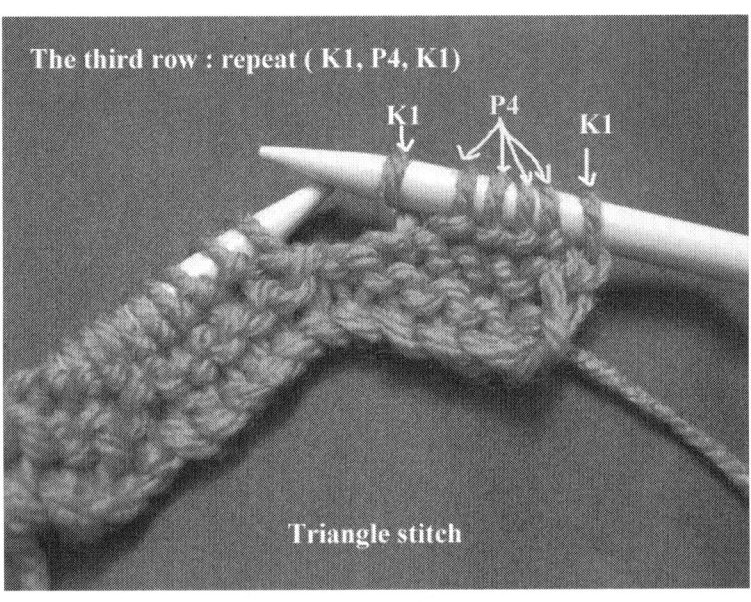

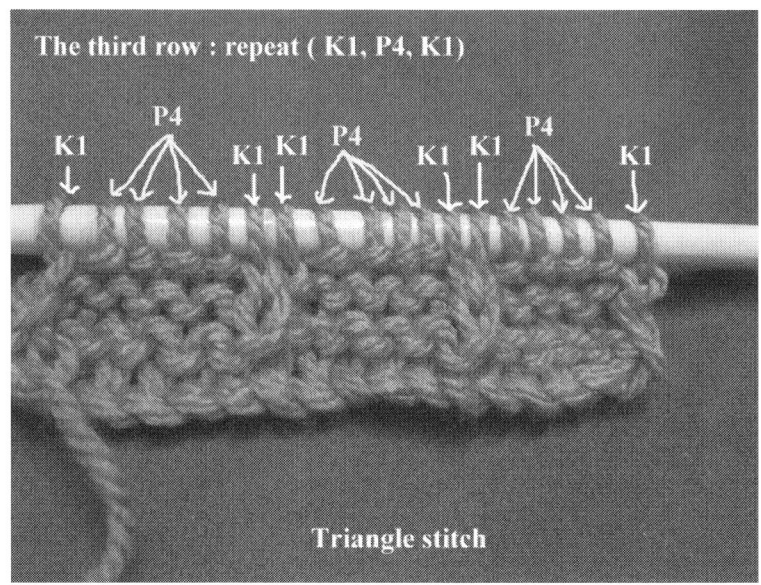

Row 4: (P2, K3, P1) repeat to the end of the row.

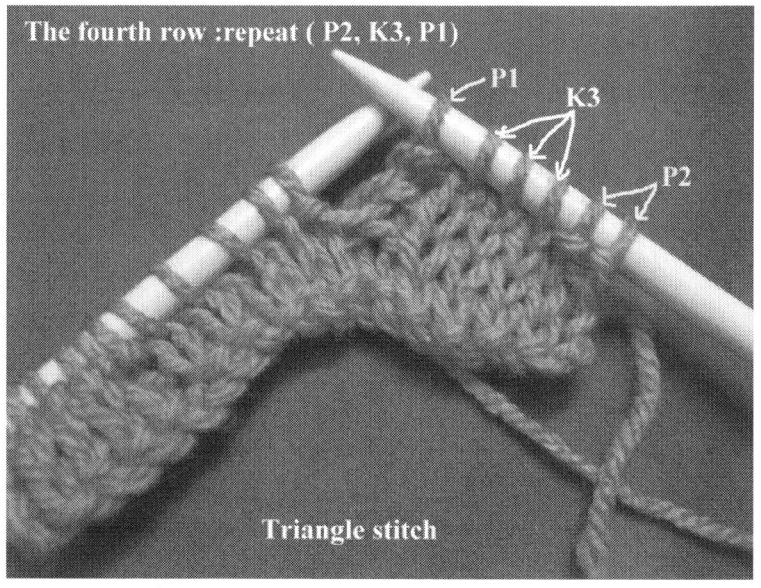

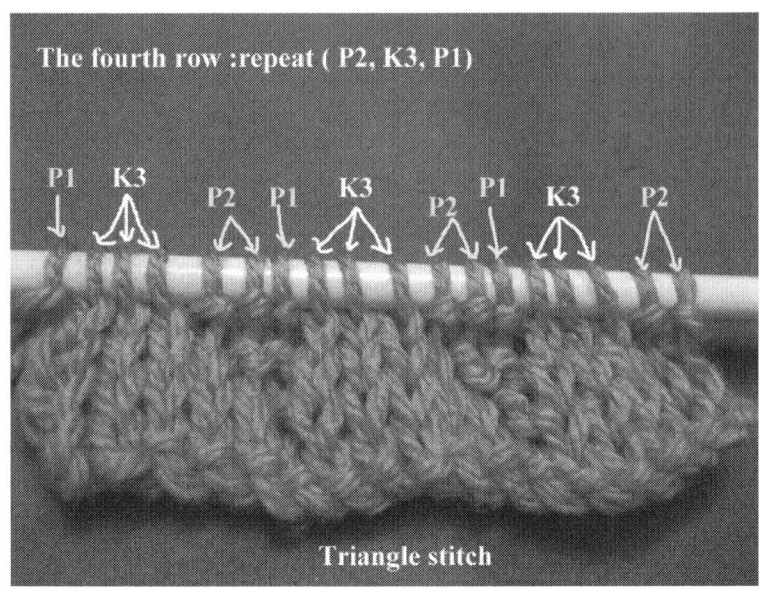

Row 5: (K1, P2, K3) repeat until the end of the row.

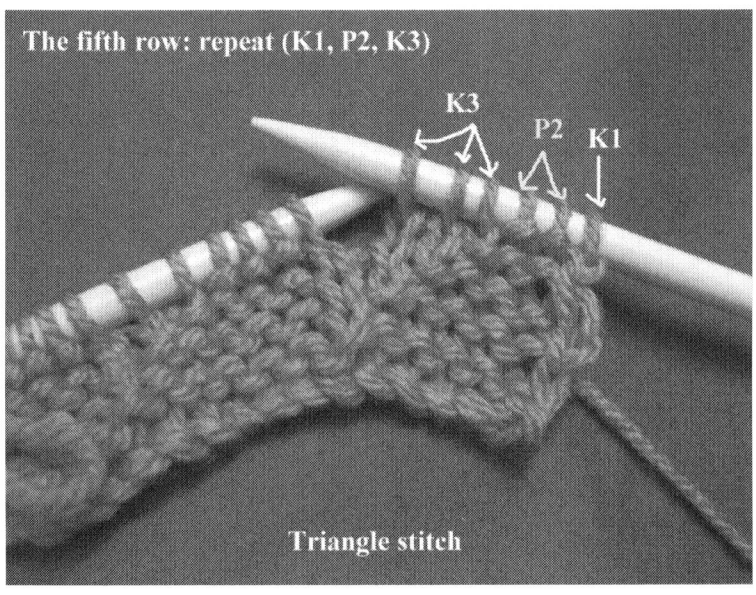

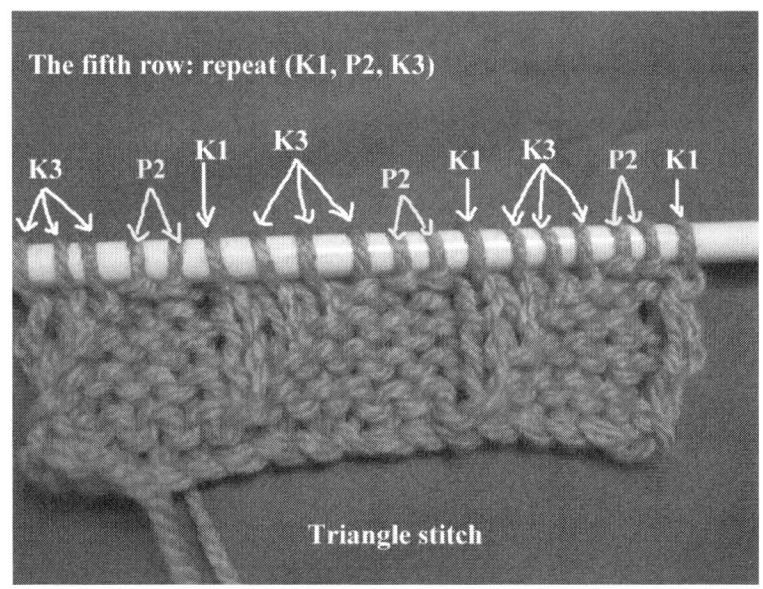

Row 6: (P4, K1, P1) repeat until the end of the row.

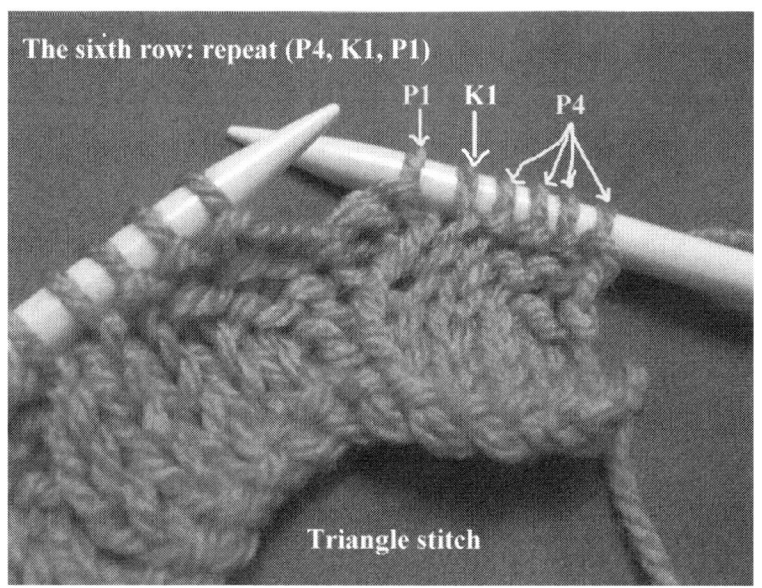

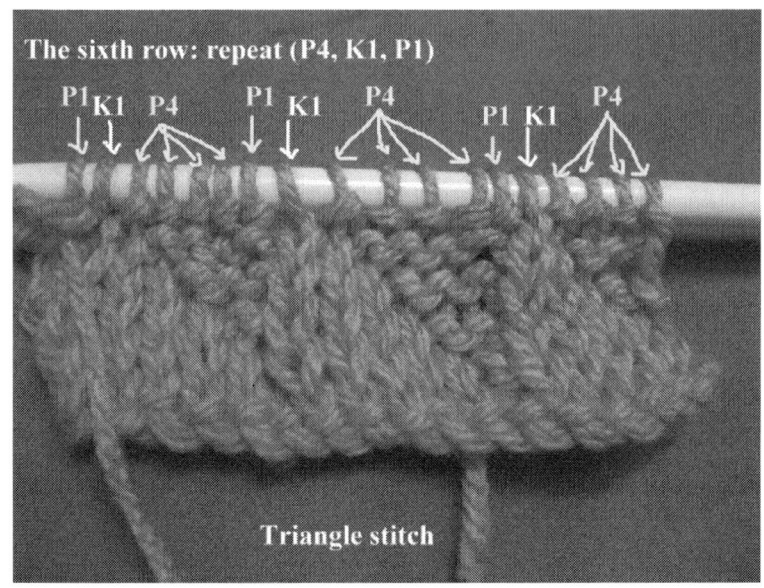

Row 7: Purl (P) all the stitches.

Row 8: (P4, K1, P1) repeat until the end of the row.

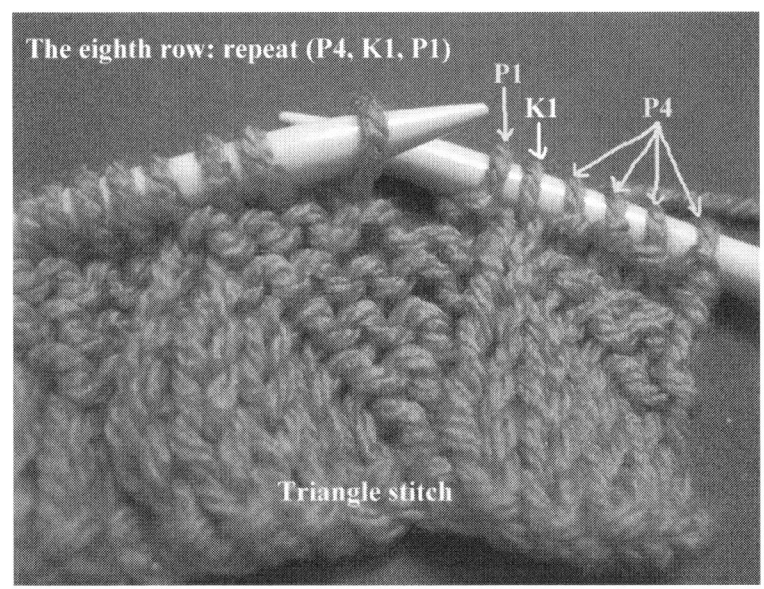

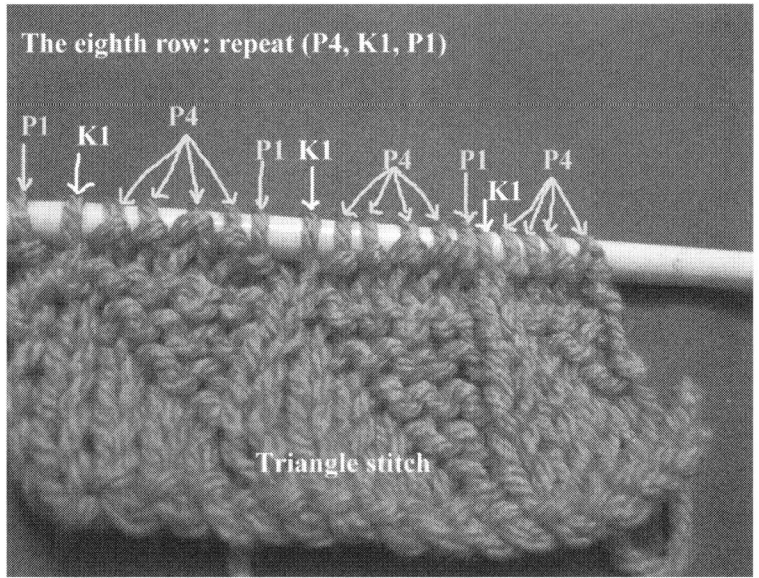

Row 9: (K1, P2, K3) repeat until the end of the row.

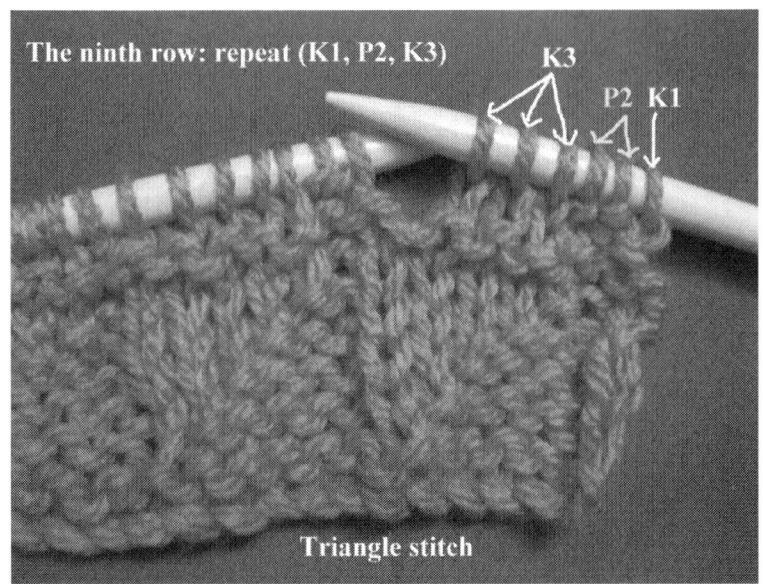

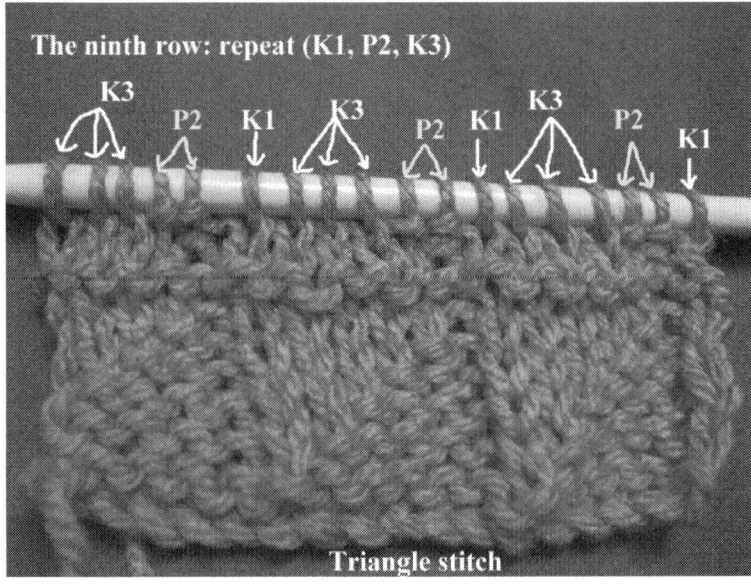

Row 10: (P2, K3, P1) repeat until the end of the row.

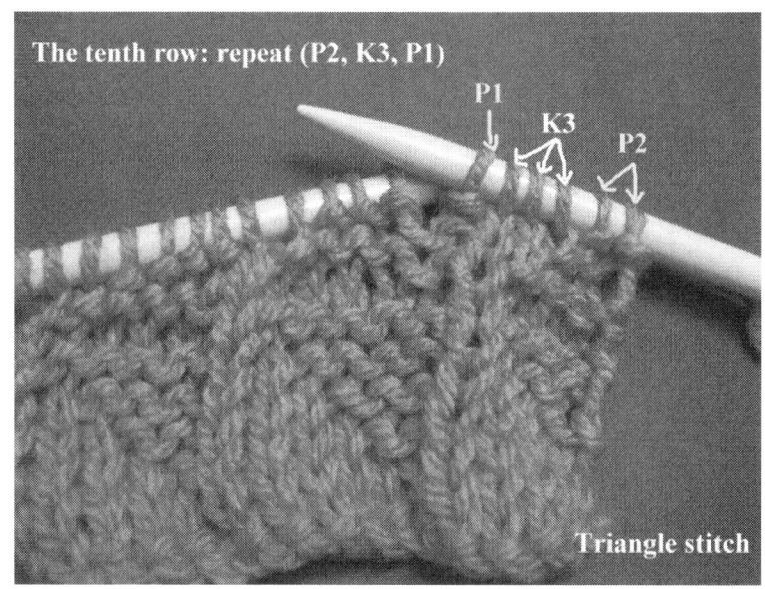

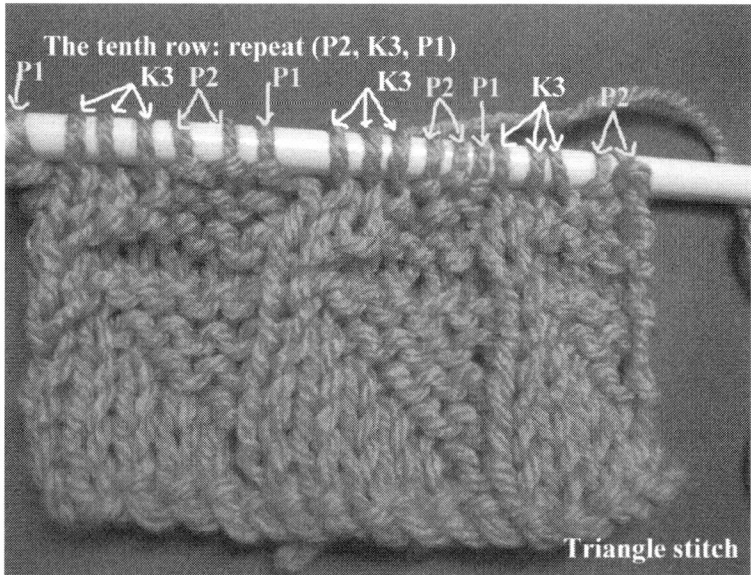

Row 11: (K1, P4, K1) repeat until the end of the row.

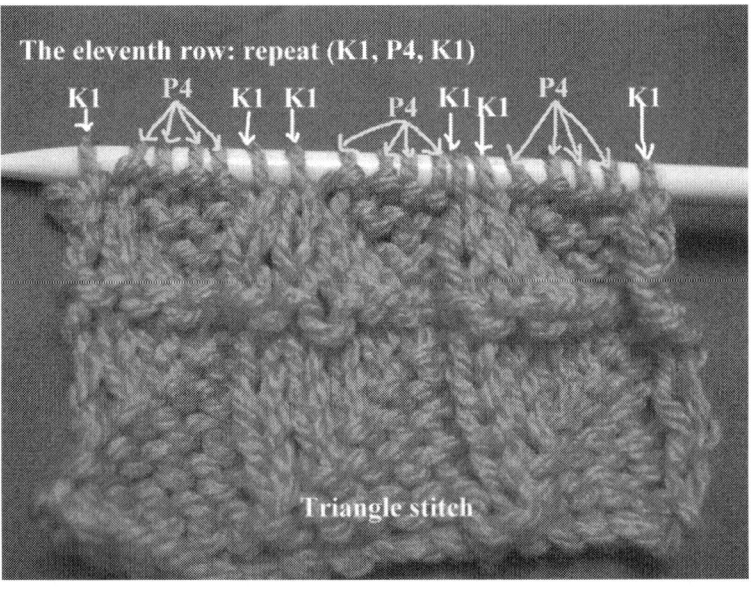

Row 12: (K5, P1) repeat until the end of the row.

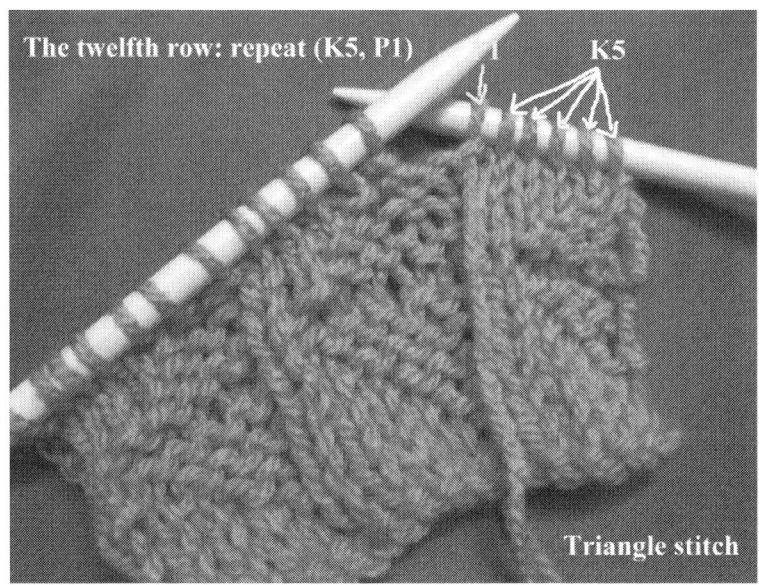

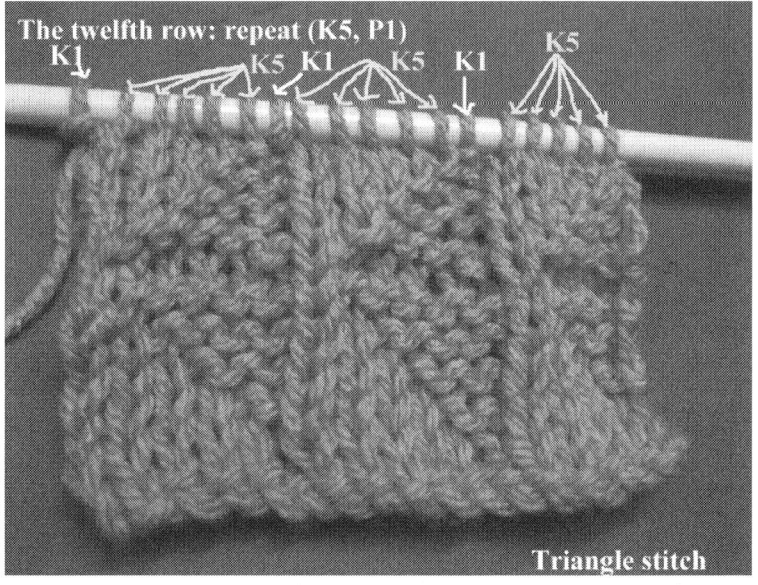

Continue the pattern, repeating the 12 rows from the first row. This chart illustrates the stitches in each row of 12 rows.

Row 1	P	P	P	P	P	P
Row 2	K	K	K	K	K	P
Row 3	K	P	P	P	P	K
Row 4	P	P	K	K	K	P
Row 5	K	P	P	K	K	K
Row 6	P	P	P	P	K	P
Row 7	P	P	P	P	P	P
Row 8	P	P	P	P	K	P
Row 9	K	P	P	K	K	K
Row 10	P	P	K	K	K	P
Row 11	K	P	P	P	P	K
Row 12	K	K	K	K	K	P

Strips Stitch

Row 1: Knit (K) all the stitches.

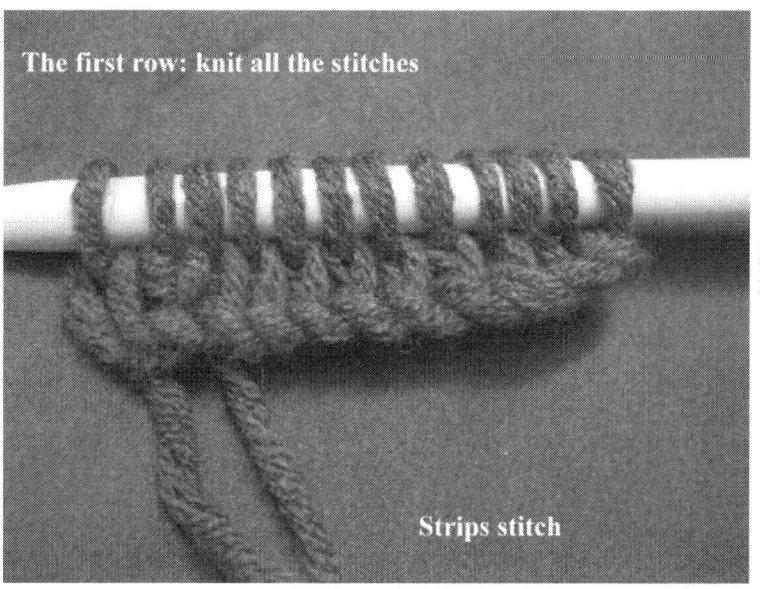

Row 2: Purl (P) all the stitches.

Row 3: Knit (K) all the stitches.

Row 4: Knit (K) all the stitches.

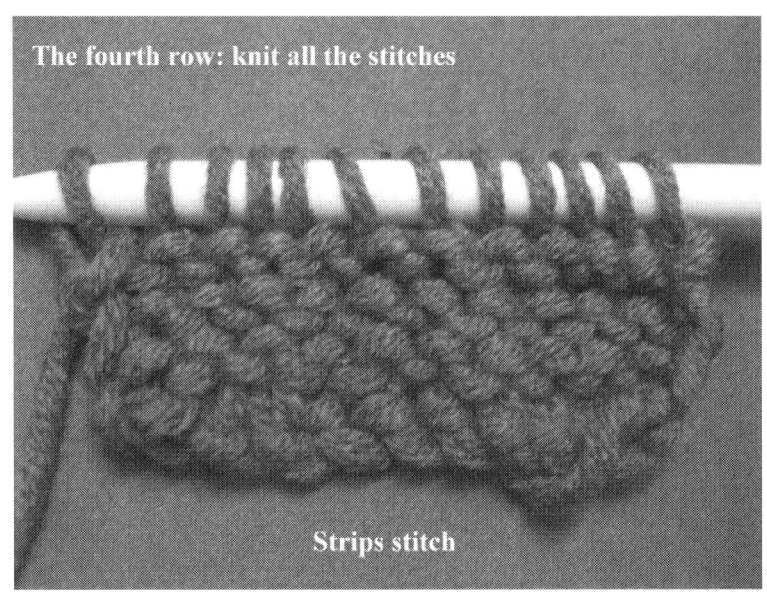

Row 5: Purl (P) all the stitches.

Row 6: Knit (K) all the stitches.

Repeat the six rows from the first row.

Row 1	k
Row 2	p
Row 3	k
Row 4	k
Row 5	p
Row 6	k

The Seed Stitch

This stitch is amazing for making scarves and baby blankets, and it does not curl.

First, cast on an even number of stitches

Row 1: (K1, P1) repeat until the end of the row.

Row 2: (P1, K1) repeat until the end of the row.

Continue doing with this manner, repeat the two rows over and over.

Row 1	k	p
Row 2	P	K

Barely Stitch

First, cast on a number of stitches that can be divided by 2, plus 2 for the edges.

Row 1: Knit (K) all the stitches.

Row 2: K1. As you knit, put the working yarn in front of your right needle.

SL1. Then cross the working yarn in front of the stitch. Put it in the back of your right-hand needle.

Rest of the row: Repeat this process until the last stitch, then knit the last stitch (K1).

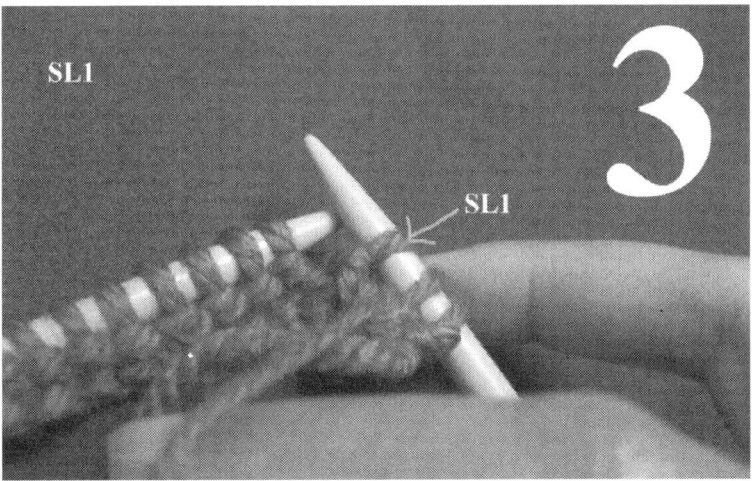

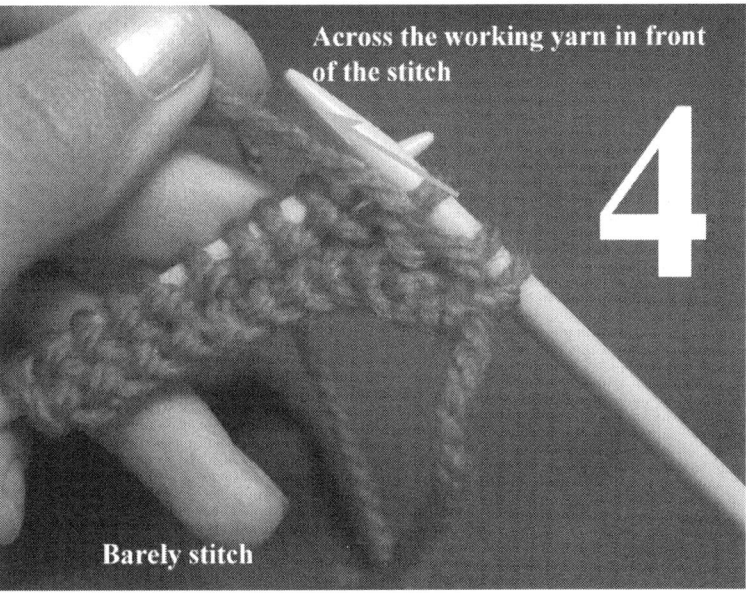

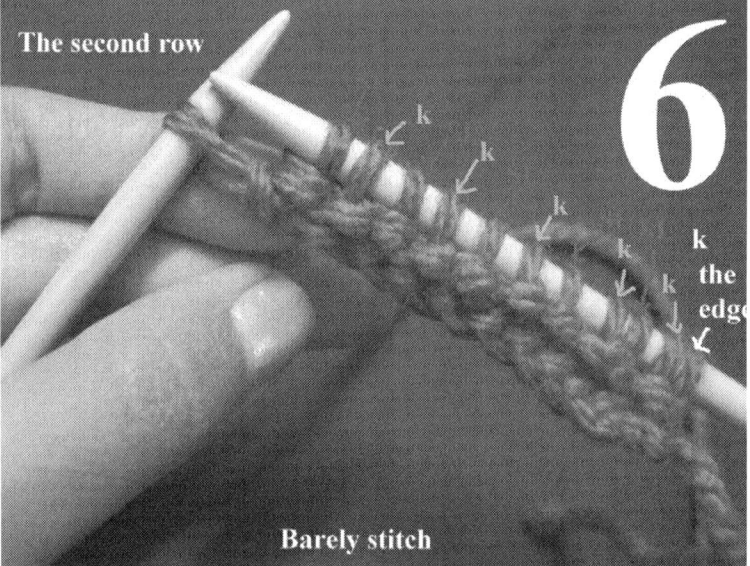

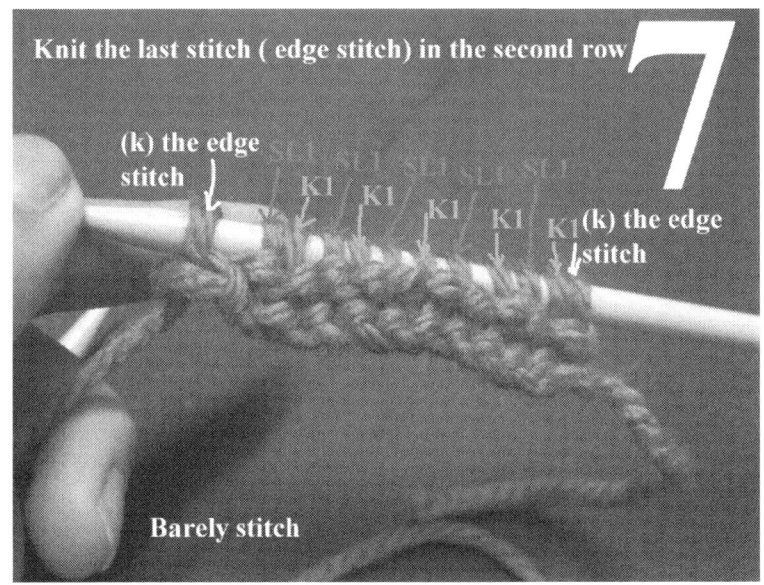

Row 3: Knit (K) all the stitches.

Row 4: K1. Bring the working yarn in front of the right-hand needle.

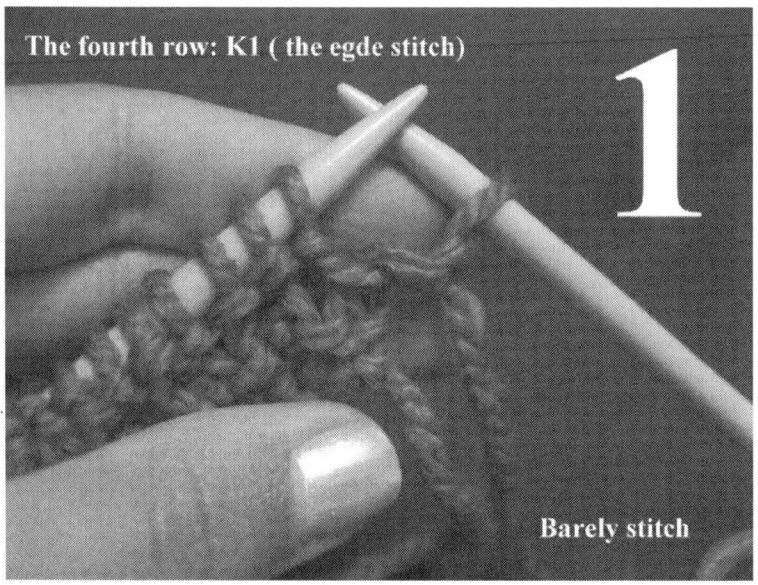

SL1, cross the working yarn in front of the stitch. Put it in the back of your right-hand needle.

K1. Repeat this process until the last stitch, then knit the last stitch (K1).

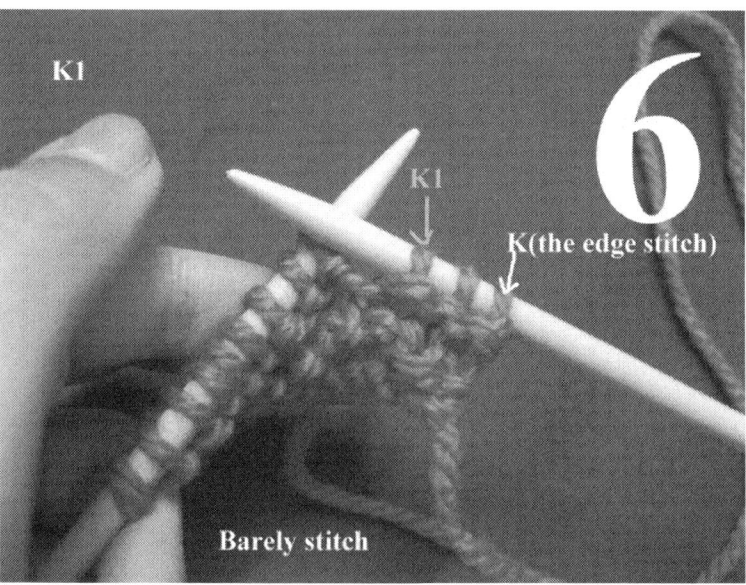

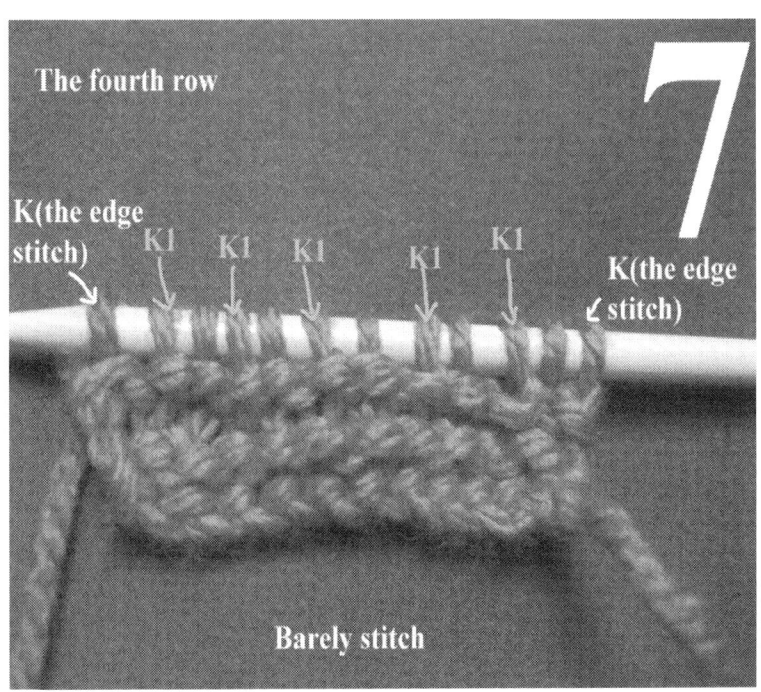

Row 1	K	K	K	K
Row 2	(K)the edge	K1 and then bring the working yarn to the front	SL1 then cross the working yarn in front of the stitch. Put it in the back of your right-hand needle	(K)the edge
Row 3	K	K	K	K
Row 4	(K)the edge	Bring The working yarn to the front then SL1.	Cross the working yarn in front of the stitch. Put it in the back of your right-hand needle, K1	(K)the edge

Cabling Stitches

You can do a lot of amazing things if you know all the tricks about cabling.

Cabling is changing the stitches order in the row by twisting them.

Basic (Braid) Cable Stitch

You have to cast on a number of stitches that can be divided by 7.

The cable consists of 4 stitches and 3 stitches on the side of it.

Row 1: The right side (P3, K4)

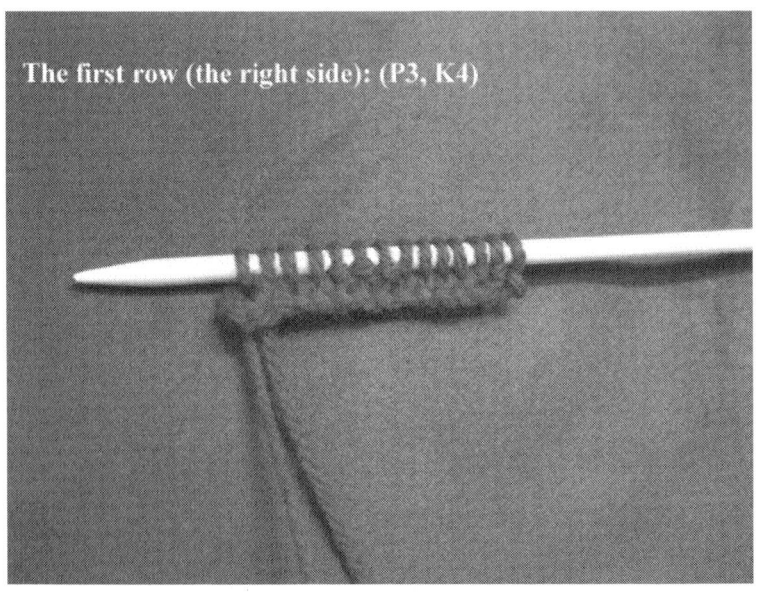

Row 2: On the wrong side (P4, K3)

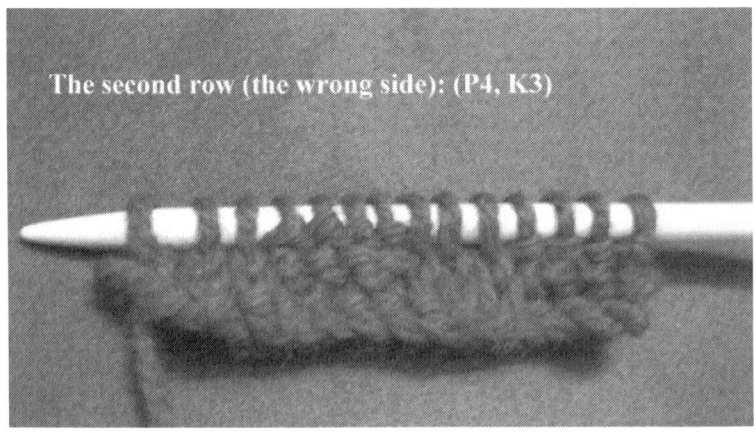

Row 3: The right side (P3, K4)

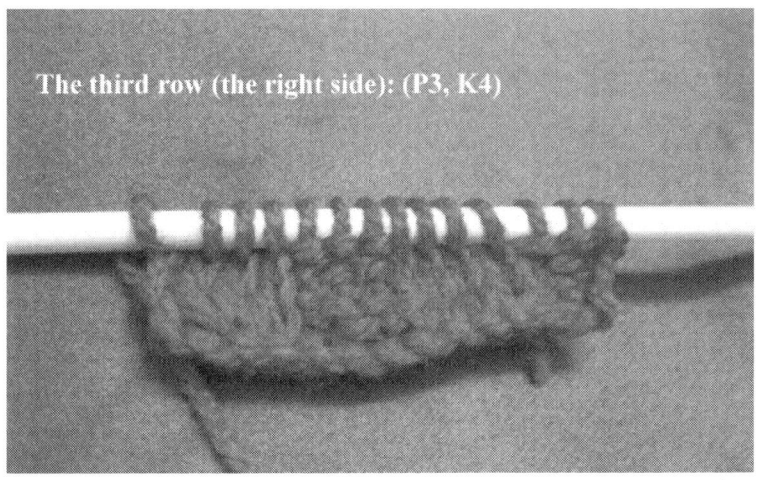

Row 4: The wrong side (P4, K3)

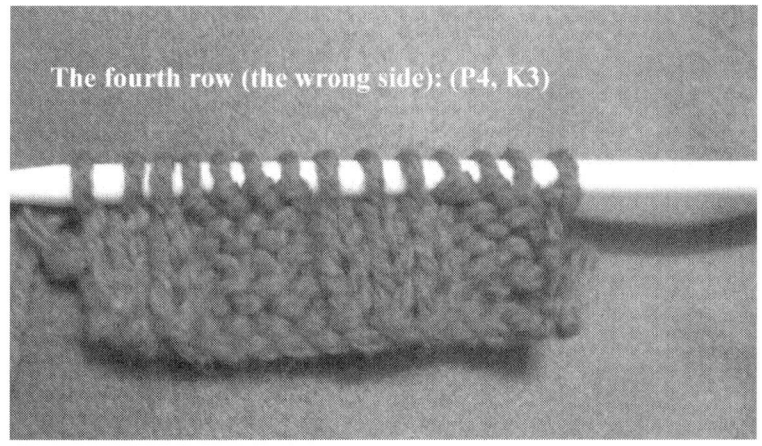

Row 5: (Picture 1) With the cable row on the right side, (P3) place the next 2 stitches on a third needle and hold to the front.

You can use one double pointed needle, or you can use a clover cable stitch holder.

(Picture 2) K2.

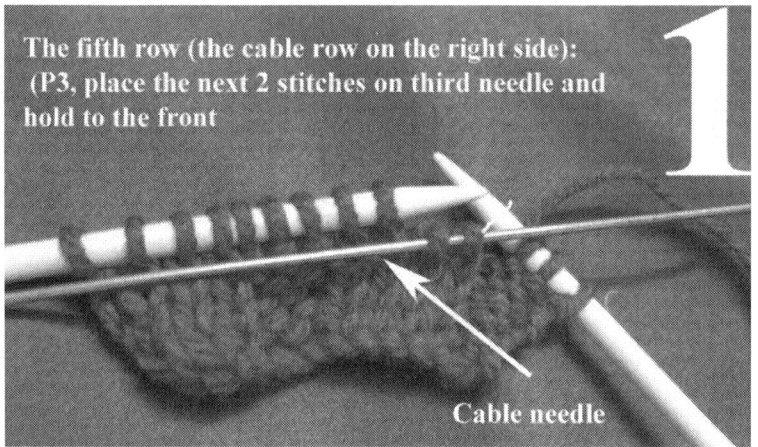

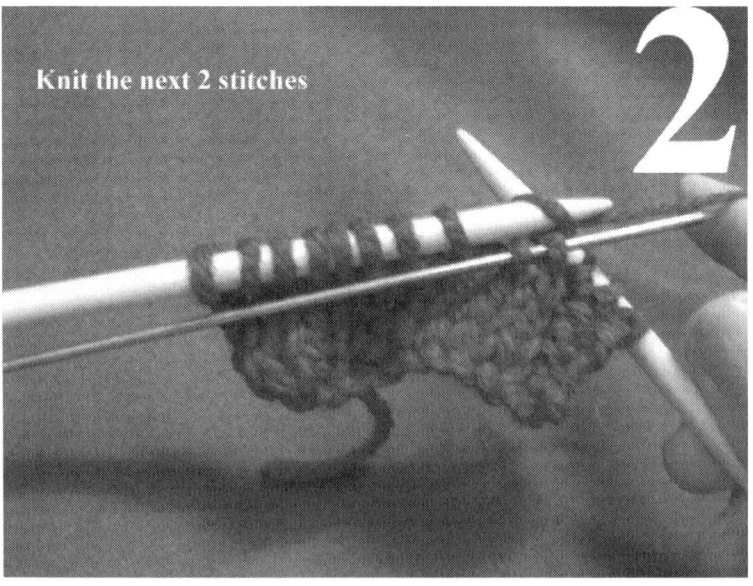

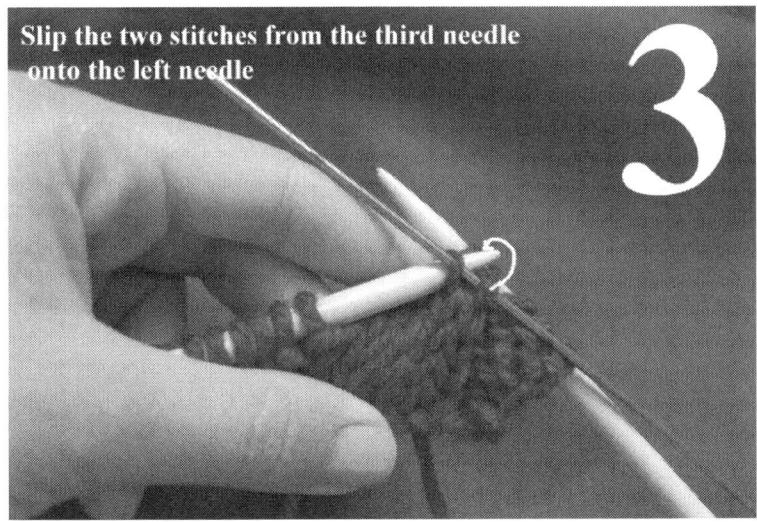

Then (Pictures 3 to 6) slip the two stitches from the third needle onto the left needle and knit them. (K2) from the third needle.

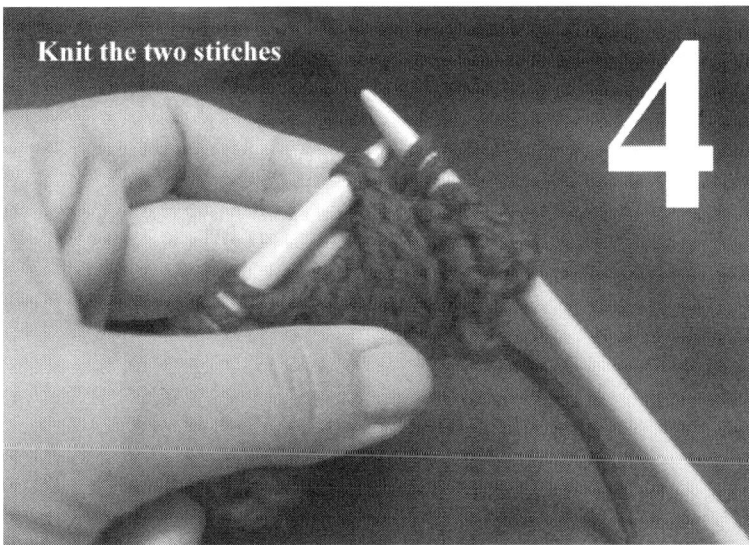

When that row is finished, it looks like this.

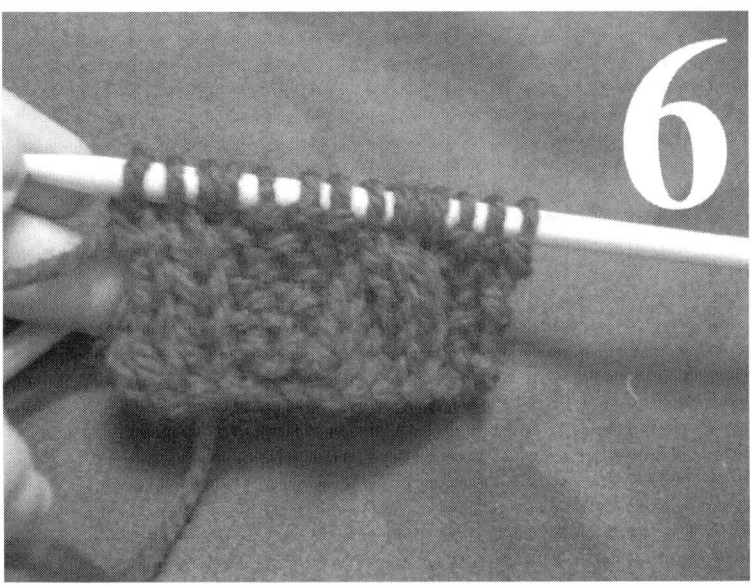

Row 6: The wrong side (P4, K3)

Row 7: The right side (P3, K4)

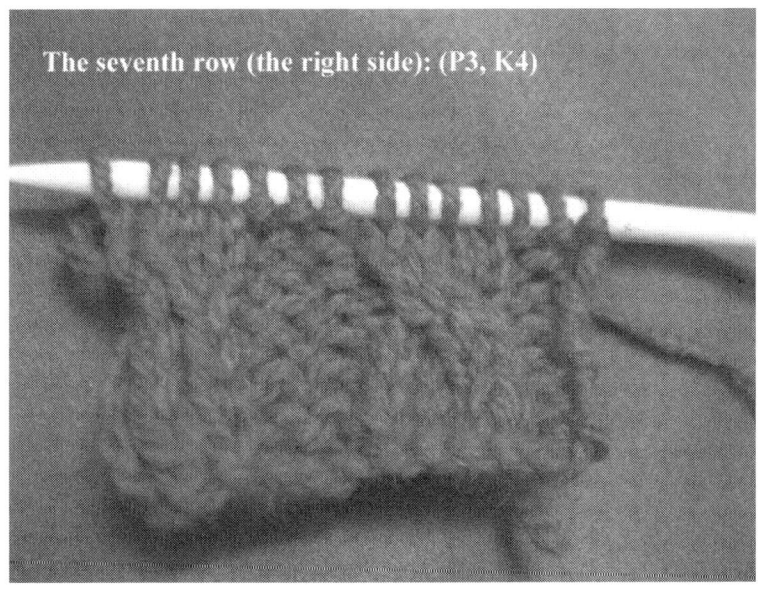

Row 8: The wrong side (P4, K3)

Row 9: The right side (P3, K4)

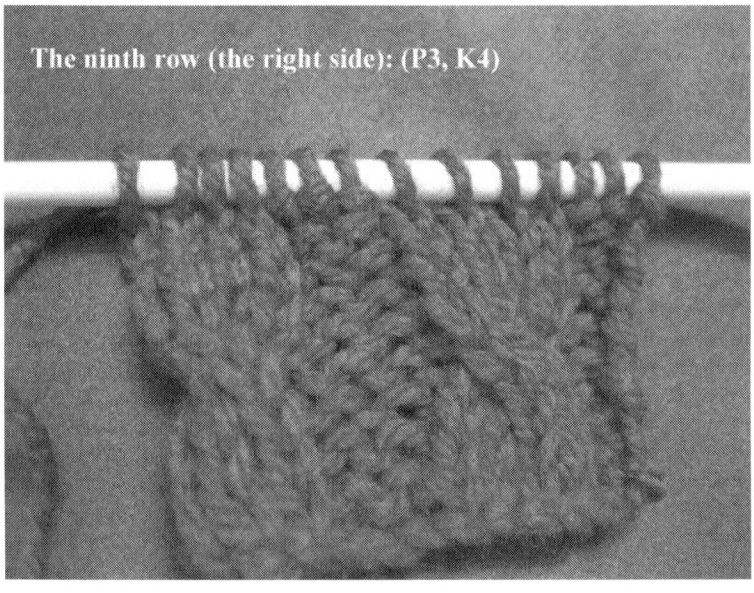

Row 10: The wrong side (P4, K3)

The tenth row (the wrong side): (P4, K3)

Row 11: With the cable row on the right side (P3). Place the next 2 stitches on the third needle and hold to the back (Picture 1).

The eleventh row (the cable row on the right side): (P3, place the next 2 stitches on third needle and hold to the back

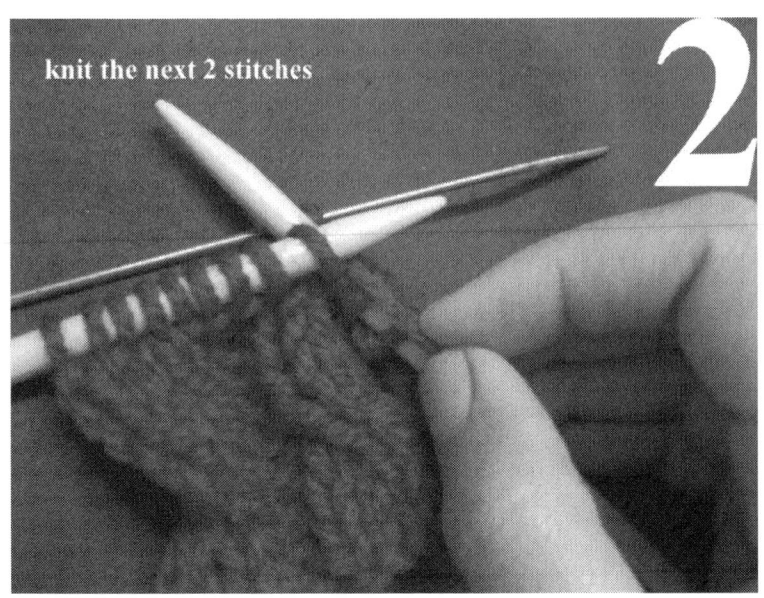

(Picture 2) K2. Then slip the two stitches from the third needle onto the left needle (Picture 3).

Knit those stitches (Picture 4) K2 from the third row (Pictures 5 and 6)

Row 12: The wrong side (P4, K3)

Continue this pattern, repeating the twelve rows from the first row.

Note: you have to knit the cable on the right side.

Now you know enough to alter this pattern. For instance, make the ninth row the first cable row. Alternate it every 10 rows. That would be repeated in Row 19 and 29, etc.

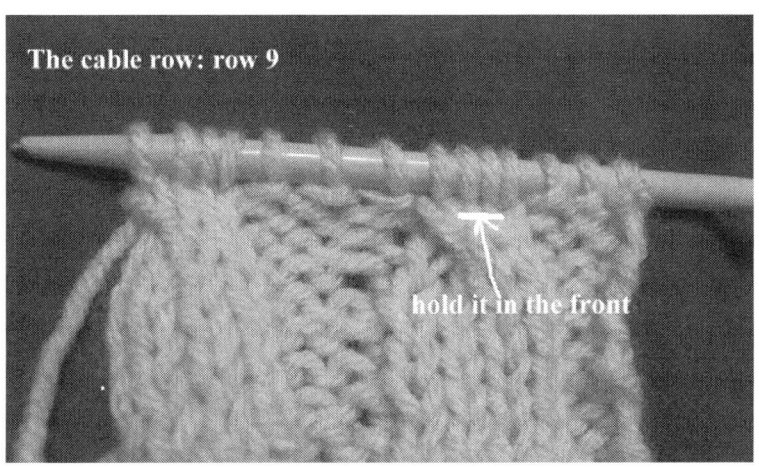

The cable row: row 9
hold it in the front

the alternate cable row : row 19
hold it in the back

You can put the third needle to the front or the back in both the fifth row and eleventh row.

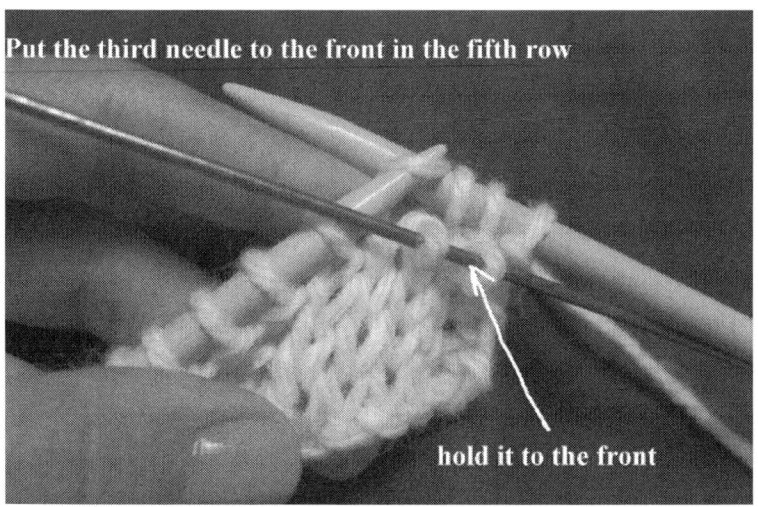

Reference the image.

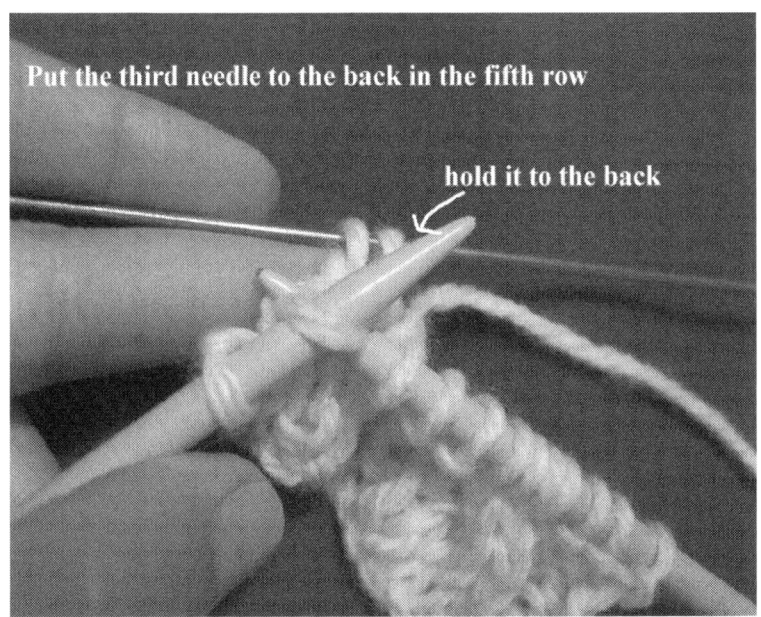

The arrow illustrates.

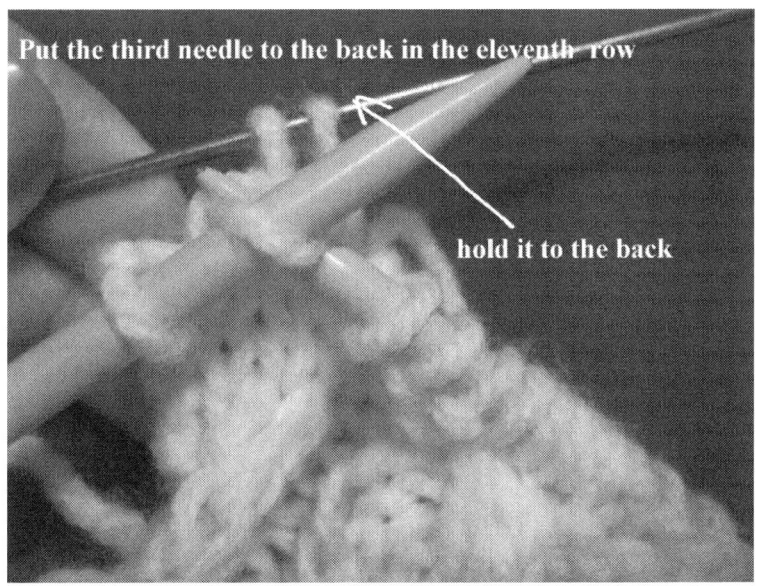

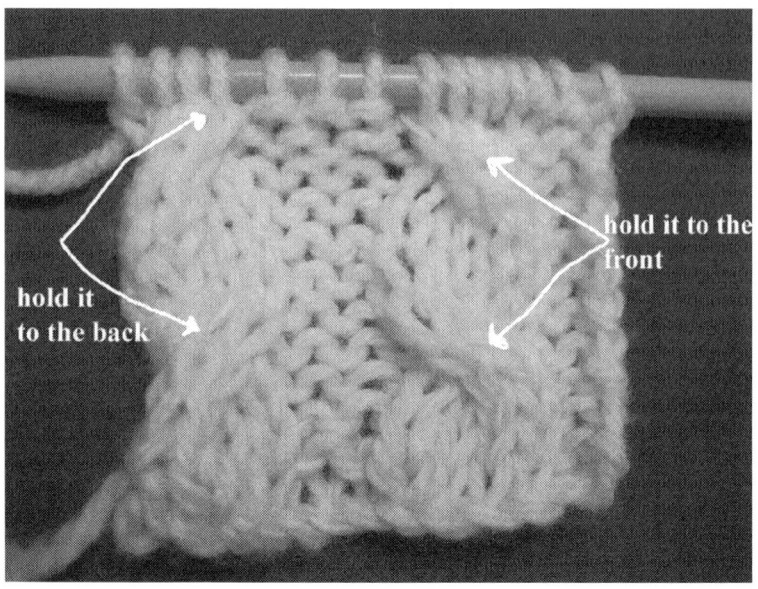

You can also make the cable from the third row and alternate it in the fifth row and in all odd rows.

Now let's do something more advanced.

Double Cable (Horseshoe) Stitch

Cast on a number of stitches that can be divided by 18. The cable consists of 12 stitches and 3 set-up stitches on each side.

Row 1: The right side (P3, K12, P3)

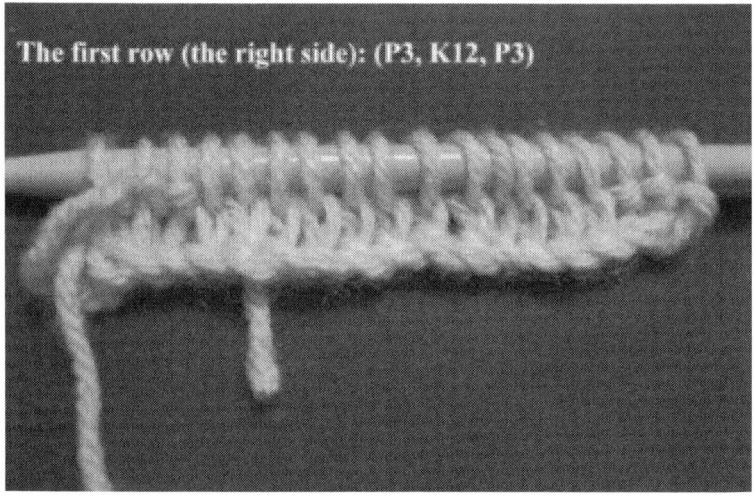

Row 2: The wrong side (K3, P12, K3)

Row 3: The right side (P3, K12, P3)

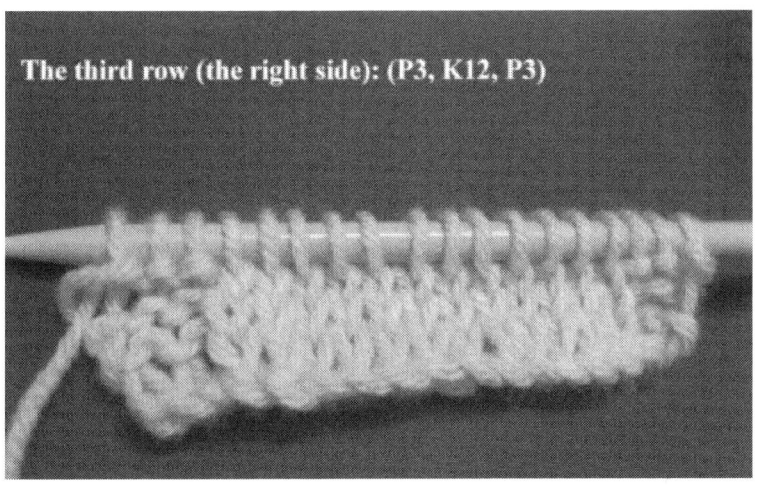

Row 4: The wrong side (K3, P12, K3)

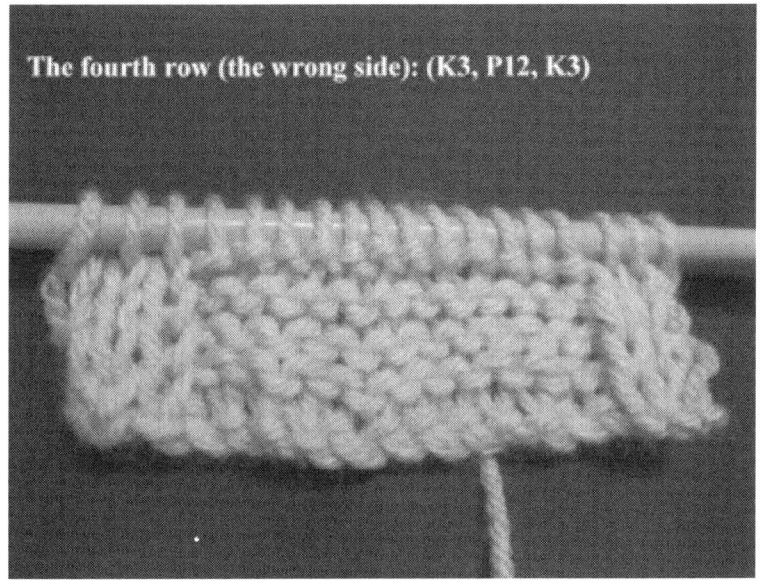

Row 5: With the cable row on the right side (P3). Place the next 3 stitches on the third needle and hold to the back (K3) (Picture 1). Slip the three stitches from the third needle onto the left needle (Picture 2).

Knit them (Picture 3).

K3 from the third needle (Picture 4). Place the next 3 stitches on the third needle and hold it to the front.

Knit the next 3 stitches (K3) (Picture 5).

(Picture 6) Slip the three stitches from the third needle onto the left needle.

Knit them (K3) from the third needle (P3) (Pictures 7 and 8).

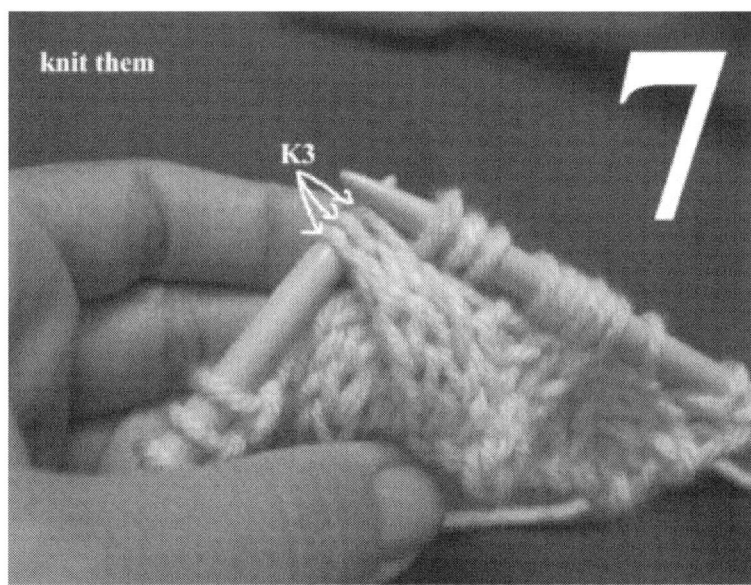

Row 6: The wrong side (K3, P12, K3)

Repeat the six rows from the first row.

This cable is oriented upwards. If you wish, you can turn it downwards. Do this by putting the third needle to the front first and alternate to the back in the next set of stitches.

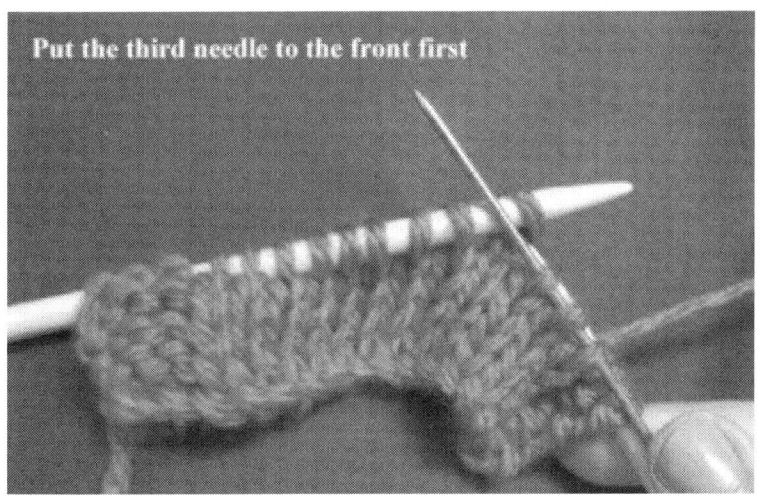

It looks like this when done.

The left cable (LPC): put the third needle to the front.

The right cable (RPC): put the third needle to the back.

Conclusion

Creating this book has been such a labor of love. I have enjoyed knitting for years, ever since I would sit next to my dear grandmother and watch her knit for hours on end.

I hope that you get the same joy from creating something from scratch with your own two hands. Once you learn the steps and stitches of knitting, you can create wonderful, special gifts for your friends and family they will cherish for years.

Be sure to take a look at my other knitting book, *DIY Knitting By Pictures Advanced Guide to Knitting Techniques, Stitches, and Patterns with Easy-to-Follow Steps and Illustrations* where you can find many complete knitting patterns.

Thank you for reading my book. Just the fact that you are also interested in knitting warms my heart. I am very happy to spread this art throughout the world!

If this book has been of benefit to you, please consider leaving a review or rating wherever you purchased this book. It would really mean so much to me. Thank you!

Made in the USA
Columbia, SC
17 November 2022

71449393R00096